Praise for Women

"I was in awe of the amount of research and devotion the author put into this book. She writes with such joy and ease and grace. Readers will be captivated by the astounding stories of Mildred, Heber, and Lula!"
— David Aretha, award-winning author and editor

"Lucky is the family that has a story-keeper who listens carefully to the elders and then curates the stories to ensure their survival. This family history is a blessing to kinfolk and professional historians alike, with its archetypal survivors, helpmeets, and rogues mean as a snake — all presented before the backdrop that was twentieth-century Georgia history. This book sets some important stories and some important precedents: the family that is honest with each other about the past is better equipped for human flourishing in the future."
— Cynthia Shearer, award-winning author of two novels set in the South, *The Wonder Book of the Air* and *The Celestial Jukebox*

Women of the Wind

A True Story of Abandonment, Abduction, and Abuse and the Women Who Survived It All

Women of the Wind

Angela Gail Griffin

Copyright © 2022 by Angela Gail Griffin

All rights reserved. No part of this publication may be reproduced, stored, or transmitted in any form or by any means without written permission of the publisher or author, except in the case of brief quotations embodied in critical articles and reviews.

This book reflects the author's transcribed conversations of experiences over time and her interpretation of some of these experiences. Some names have been changed to protect the privacy of individuals. Some events have been compressed, and some dialogue has been recreated.

Published by Clover Street Books

For more information or to contact the author,
visit www.womenofthewind.com.

ISBN (paperback): 979-8-9865912-0-9
ISBN (ebook): 979-8-9865912-1-6

Editors: David Aretha and Andrea Vanryken
Book cover and interior design:
Christy Day, Constellation Book Services

Printed in the United States of America

For my mother

"I realize now that my memories and Aunt Bell's memories may pass down to generations to come, your children's children, and their children and on because that's a keepsake."
—Irma Gail Hodge, 2006

Irma Gail Hodge (1927–2013)

Contents

Preface	1

Part I: After THEY TOOK HER BABY — 7

Taken in the Wind	9
Trapped in the Whirlwind	19
Into the Winds of Freedom	29
The Gail Force Wind	35
Lost in the Wind	49
A Welcomed Breeze	61

Part II: LULA FIGHTS BACK — 73

The Children in the Sawpit	75
Good Fortune	81
A Windfall	89
A Hurricane Is Coming	97
Gusts of Disgust	103
Winds of Change	111
A Blast from the Past	119
The Lights Like People Have	127
The Disabilities of the Plaintiff	139
A Mother's Love	147
Epilogue	155
Acknowledgments	167

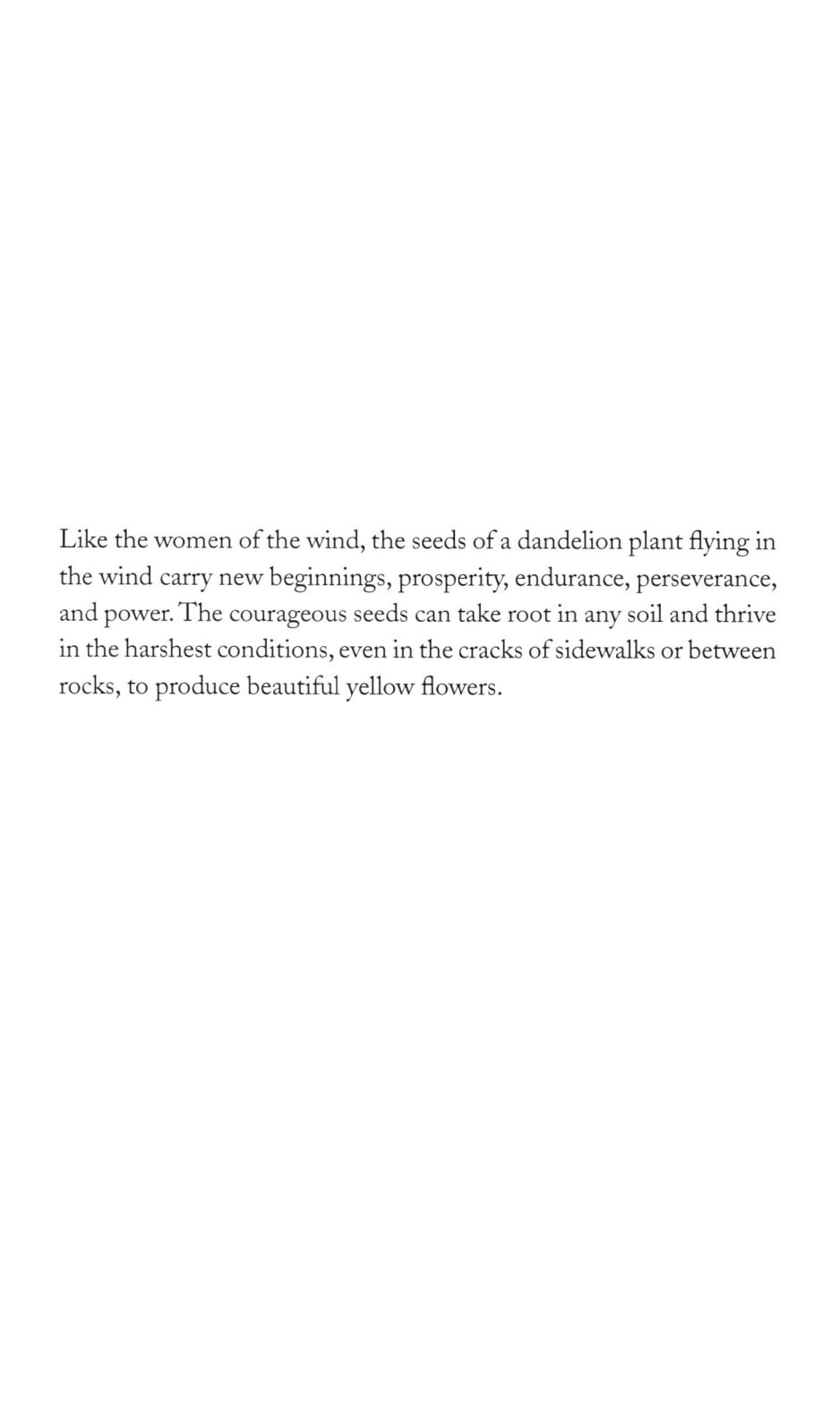

Like the women of the wind, the seeds of a dandelion plant flying in the wind carry new beginnings, prosperity, endurance, perseverance, and power. The courageous seeds can take root in any soil and thrive in the harshest conditions, even in the cracks of sidewalks or between rocks, to produce beautiful yellow flowers.

Preface

DO YOU EVER WONDER IF FAMILIES pass down stories about their lives and the lives of family members who came before them? In today's fast-paced, technology-driven world where current events and social media consume people, probably not. But in my world, my mother passed down childhood memories and tales of her mother and grandmother to me. And although my mother's stories drifted in and out of my mind, they remained planted firmly in my soul.

During the 1990s, I realized that I should pen my mother's words so that others could hear them, and I dreamed of someday writing a book based on her memories. I am not sure if I was divinely chosen as the one to impart my mother's family history, or if I was the one most fascinated and enthralled with it, the one who would not forget it, the one who could not get it out of her mind.

In the new millennium, a search for evidence to support my mother's recollections led me to the courthouse in Wayne County, Georgia, where I found a treasure trove of court documents that proved without any doubt what my mother told me was true. For the next ten years, with command of the internet and its infinite source of information, I gained more knowledge related to my mother's story. I soon transformed into a pack rat, hoarding and protecting in a small, fireproof safe copied court documents and downloaded internet files.

For another ten years evidence that my mother's memories were accurate and truthful remained untouched in the safe, and I continued dreaming about writing this book until now. So, when is "now"? Now is 2020, and I must quarantine because of the Covid-19 pandemic. Now I have all the time needed to write, uninterrupted by the constraints of a career or a busy family life. Now I acknowledge that I am the third-generation storyteller in my mother's family, following my Aunt Bell and my mother, and I feel compelled to pass on their stories. Now I am happily married, retired, and I choose to spend my time at home writing with or without a pandemic.

I am a homebody. I always have been. It must be in my DNA to be one. My paternal grandmother, Mattie, was a homebody and a writer. Settled and content in her home office after she retired, Mattie authored a column for her local newspaper entitled "Golden Treasures."

As I begin composing my "golden treasure," I am not alone. I share my office with my twenty-year-old cat, isolated in it for almost a year after her failing kidneys caused her to have accidents all over my house.

My cat and I spend most days together in my office now; I write, and she sleeps. I have an intuition that she will live until I finish the first draft; I pray that she does, but her health declines every day.

When I rescued my office mate from a feral litter in 2000, my interest in my great-grandmother, Miss Lou, a dominant character in my mother's stories, peaked. My new kitten's wild, untamable personality reminded me of my great-grandmother, so I chose to name her "Lou," suitable for males or females since I was unsure of her sex.

Coincidentally, my cat and her namesake share the same propensity to spew foul language, a fact I learned after Lou's first trip to the veterinarian for an examination. After taking a good look at my little ball of fur, the vet lifted it high into the air and announced, "It's a girl!" and added a metaphor for her loud, distinctive, angry meow, "Her language is nasty!"

With my hissing, growling, fowl-speaking feline back home, I called my mother to report that Lou's full name was "Miss Lou." My mother replied with an incredulous tone in her voice, "Well, you certainly chose the right name. My Grandma Lou cussed like a sailor!"

I find it serendipitous that the two Miss Lous would converge in the room where one lies beside me, and the other's portrait hangs on the wall over my shoulder, serving as inspirations for this book. If I feel any hesitation or self-doubt while writing, I look at them for reassurance, and they both hiss in my ear, "Write the damn book. It's time!"

My cat, Miss Lou, named after Lula, remained by my side every day for six months while I wrote this book. She crossed the rainbow bridge three days after I finished the rough draft.

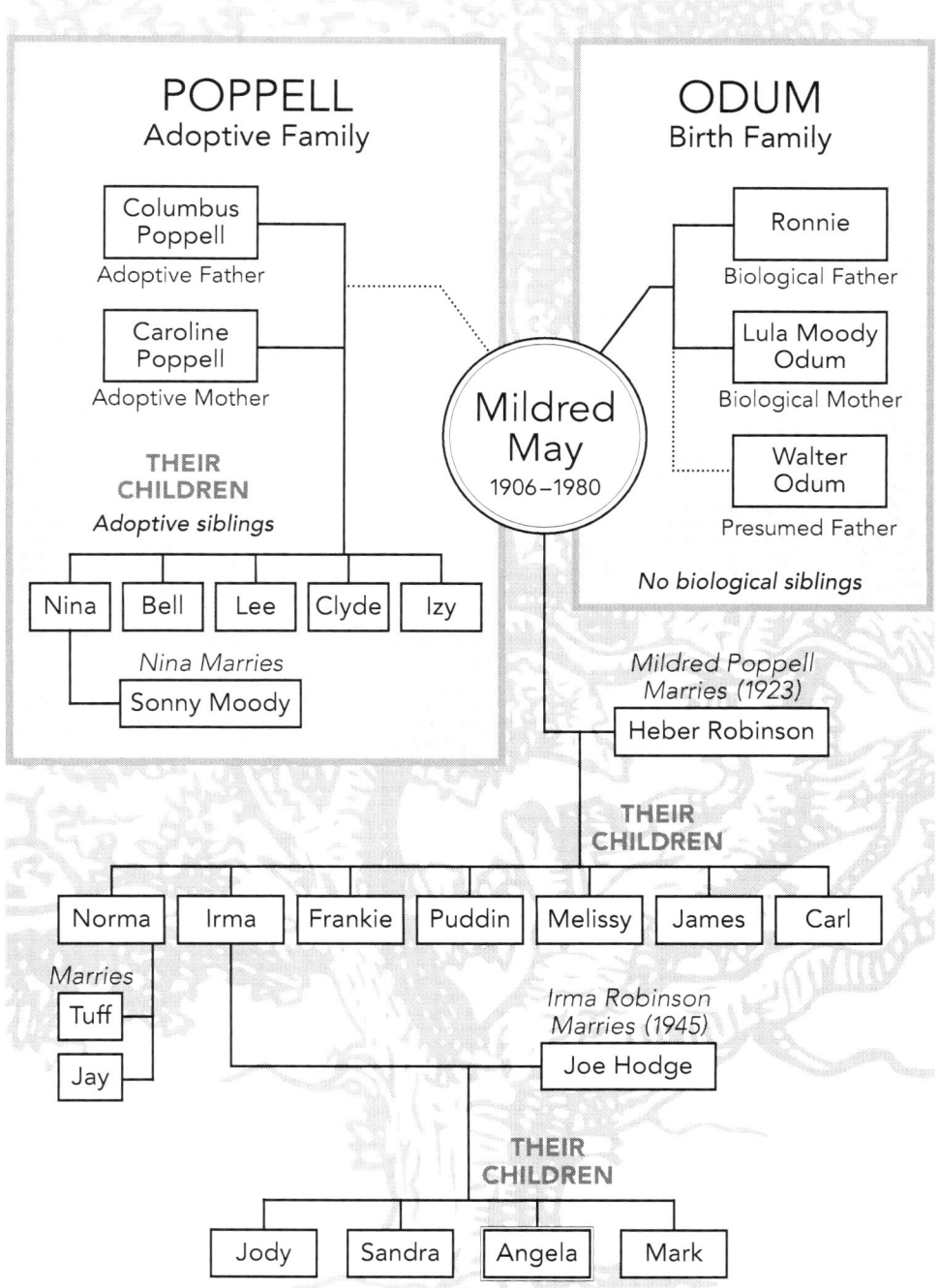

PART I
After They Took Her Baby

Mildred May on the Robinson farm in 1946.

CHAPTER 1
Taken in the Wind

CAROLINE POPPELL LIVED an uncomplicated life in the rural countryside of South Georgia. That is, until that unforgettable day in 1906 when her good friend Victoria suddenly appeared one Saturday morning with an urgent message and begged for help. Caroline knew something was wrong when the horse pulling Victoria's buggy raced up to her house and abruptly stopped. Before Caroline could invite her inside, Victoria blurted out something about a baby in trouble and needing help.

Seated in her single carriage, her hands still on the reins, Victoria shared with Caroline that her daughter-in-law Lula did not regularly feed her severely malnourished newborn and left the child alone for hours, sometimes overnight. Victoria told Caroline that her son was unaware of Lula's ill-treatment of the baby until she wrote him and urged him to return from medical school immediately. Victoria pleaded with Caroline to help her and her son seize and hide the infant, or the child may not live much longer.

Caroline had known Victoria for years and had never seen her so panicked and saw no need to question the truthfulness of her story; Caroline trusted her old friend. Without hesitation, Caroline assured Victoria that she and her oldest daughter, twenty-year-old Nina, would be on time at the child's home the following day. Caroline Poppell would roll over anyone who got in her way when her friends and family needed help, earning her the nickname "Tank" after World War I. She was the ideal ally for Victoria's rescue mission.

As discussed, the women arrived at Lula's house with two fresh horses and their best carriage, prepared for a fight if the scheme to lure the mother away from home failed. But there was no confrontation; Lula was not there. A servant girl let the women in the house and guided them to the nursery.

Caroline and Nina heard only their footsteps as they approached the baby's cradle; the child made no sound. The sight of the newborn's motionless, emaciated body shocked Caroline, and she wondered if the infant would survive the short journey to her home. The baby did not wake or react when Caroline wrapped it in blankets in preparation for the trip. The child's shallow breaths were the only sign of life.

Tearing into the piercing February winds, emboldened by their successful mission, Caroline and Nina hurriedly vanished like bandits with the baby. Caroline cradled the helpless infant under her coat to keep it warm while Nina led the horses home.

Caroline's husband, Columbus, and the other Poppell children gathered by a roaring fire, anxiously awaiting Caroline's and Nina's return with the baby. The family had no time to grasp the seriousness of the child's condition and were not prepared for what they were about to see. When Caroline un-swaddled the baby, the Poppell family stared in disbelief at the poor infant who weighed only a few pounds as she lay listlessly in a deep sleep in Caroline's arms.

The child was born full-term six weeks earlier, on January 6, 1906, and named Mildred May by her birth mother. At six weeks, Mildred May weighed less than she did at birth, and Nina noticed that Mildred May's wrist was no bigger than her father's ring finger. At Nina's insistence, Columbus slid his wedding band with ease over the sleeping child's hand but quickly removed it, fearing it might get stuck.

With Columbus's ring safely off Mildred May's wrist and back on his finger, Caroline bathed and dressed the new baby, hoping to wake her, but it would be the next day before Mildred May opened her eyes. And when she did, her raging screams bewildered and frightened the Poppells, who desperately wanted to help her. But Mildred May did not stop crying and shaking and refused to suckle a bottle.

Caroline and Nina took turns rocking and singing to the distressed baby girl they held close to their chest, attempting to soothe her. But nothing comforted the child until, on the third day, desperate to get the infant to drink and relax, Caroline brought a "wet nurse" into her home to feed the pitiful child. Caroline breathed a sigh of relief when Mildred May latched onto the lactating woman and began to nurse.

For weeks the routine never changed; Caroline and Nina rocked and sang to the screaming, trembling infant between feedings with the wet nurse, who, along with her baby, had moved into the Poppell home. Before long, Mildred May settled into a regular schedule of sleeping and nursing, and eventually, Columbus's wedding band was too small for Mildred May's wrist.

Days became weeks, and weeks became months without hearing a word from Lula, Mildred May's birth mother. When the Poppells heard that Lula had left town, remarried, and started a new life, they believed that she was gone for good. They had all fallen in love with Mildred May and had no intentions of surrendering her to Lula if she ever returned for her.

And that's how Mildred May, my grandmother, became a dear member of the Poppell family. Born an only child, Mildred May gained five siblings when the Poppells rescued her: Nina, Bell, Lee, Clyde, and Izy. Still in their early forties, Caroline and Columbus had no problem raising one more child.

Bell was fifteen years old when Mildred May joined her family and was old enough to remember every detail of Mildred May's arrival. Bell recalled that her new sister was like a doll, a toy for her family to cherish and adore. But she also remembered how fragile her baby doll sister was when Caroline and Nina brought her home. Bell never forgot how small Mildred May was, how her body shook uncontrollably, and how she wailed in pain for days. The sight of her father's wedding band fitting like a bracelet on Mildred May's tiny wrist seared into Bell's memory, and she vowed to keep an eye on her precious little sister for the rest of her life.

Mildred May's childhood with the Poppells was a blessed one. Caroline and Columbus were loving parents, and Nina and Bell became Mildred May's second and third mothers. Izy, only four years older than

Mildred May, attended school with her. But it was Bell who emerged as Mildred May's closest sibling. It was Bell who Mildred May clung to during hard times, and it was Bell who later became the favorite aunt of Mildred May's children.

Bell and her Poppell family lived in Odum, Georgia, a small community about seventy-five miles southwest of Savannah. At one time, Columbus's father, James A. Poppell, "Jim," owned most of the land that is now the city of Odum.

Hazel Dean Overstreet fondly remembered Jim in an article, "Echoes Of The Past—Odum, Georgia," she wrote for the 1985 Odum Homecoming program:

> Mr. Poppell owned a large store at that time, which sold everything from whiskey to trace chains. He was a very generous old fellow and folks recall hearing how he used to "set" all his customers up to a "drink" from the cider barrel, which he kept filled at all times. It is also told that Mr. Poppell, seeing an honest conscientious young man trying to get ahead, would, out of the generosity of his heart, give that young man a farm or a strip of woodland...

Columbus Poppell, called "Lum" by his friends and family, obviously inherited his father Jim's generous, caring heart when he opened it to a neglected, unwanted child and accepted Mildred May and loved her. Just as his father welcomed all who came to his store, Columbus welcomed Mildred May into his home.

The Poppells were a close-knit family whose cheerful household bustled with activity. Lum and his oldest son Lee supported the family by farming while Caroline prepped and prepared the meals; there was always plenty of food in the Poppell home. The firstborn, Nina, affectionately called "Miss Nin" by her students and "Aunt Nin" by her nieces, contributed to the household income by teaching music, playing the organ, and sewing. She and Bell were excellent seamstresses and tailored the family's clothes.

But it wasn't long after Mildred May joined the family that it grew smaller and smaller when Lee left home, and tragically, Columbus, the only father Mildred May would ever know, died. Without Lum and Lee to provide food from the farm, fifty-year-old Caroline depended on Nina's teaching income to support her and her children.

Only a few years after Columbus's death, there were three fewer mouths to feed when Clyde, Izy, and Mildred May married, leaving only Nina and Bell with Caroline. Caroline's two oldest daughters became the family spinsters, content to live unmarried with their mother and take care of her. But at the age of thirty-nine, Nina married, and she, too, was gone.

Bell was the only child still living at home when uterine cancer took fifty-eight-year-old Caroline's life. Losing her mother was hardest for Bell, who had no prospects for marriage and had nowhere to go when Caroline died. For the first time in her life, Bell was alone, and she missed her mother.

Thankfully, her older sister Nina and her new husband, Sonny, a prominent, twice-widowed businessman living in the nearby community of Brentwood, invited Bell to live with them. Nina and Bell were elated to be united in Sonny's home, but Bell's time there would be short. Only seven years into his marriage with Nina, Sonny contracted blood poisoning from a small cut on his hand, developed pneumonia, and died in 1931.

Because Sonny willed his home and farmland to his thirteen surviving children, Nina and Bell could not remain in Brentwood. They had to find somewhere else to go, and it wouldn't take long. Their cousin owned several houses, and offered one of them to Nina and Bell rent-free in Odum. With income from Sonny's businesses and a car he left Nina, she and Bell lived comfortably after Sonny's death.

My mother Irma, Mildred May's second child, spent summers with her Aunt Bell during her childhood, and after my mother married, she continued visiting Aunt Bell, bringing her children along. I remember spending time at Aunt Bell's little white house in the country with my mother and little brother. I can close my eyes and see Aunt Bell smiling and waving to us from the front porch as we arrived, her white hair neatly pinned back at the neckline, wearing one of the simple cotton dresses she made.

Mildred May's two youngest daughters, my mother's sisters, nicknamed Puddin and Melissy, also remember dropping by Aunt Bell's house with their older sister Norma. While at Aunt Bell's one day, eight-year-old Puddin thought it would be fun to give her five-year-old sister a ride down Aunt Bell's well. When Puddin instructed Melissy to sit in the water bucket, Melissy stretched up on her tiptoes, threw a rock into the well's dark hole, noted how long before she heard a splash, and said, "Why don't you get in the bucket?" to which Puddin replied, "I'm not getting in the bucket. You get in the bucket."

"I'm not getting in the bucket, and you can't make me!" Melissy retorted.

"Well, I'm not getting in it either."

Since neither girl relented, they both lived to tell the "Standoff at the Well" story.

Aunt Bell's well also attracted my five-year-old brother Mark, who had never seen a well or a hand pump. Mark entertained himself by lifting the handle up and down repeatedly, amazed that water flowed from the spout each time he pumped the handle. I was not as enthralled with the well as my brother or my aunts; I remember being more interested in the outhouse. Of course, it didn't take seven-year-old me long to figure out what it was and proclaim that I was never "going" in it!

All of Mildred's children and grandchildren were fond of their Aunt Bell and have cherished memories of her and her simple life in the country. When my mother, Mark, and I were with Aunt Bell, she often prepared a whole chicken for us. Cousin Joan remembers watching Aunt Bell ring one's neck, pluck it, and boil it. Because Aunt Bell killed the chickens for our dinners before we arrived, I am unscarred by the memory of seeing the hen I was eating strutting around hours before.

But what stands out in my memory about Aunt Bell is her hearing aid and the long wire attached to the battery tucked into her dress pocket. It confused me; I had never seen anyone with a wire coming out of their ear and I wondered if it was painful. But that was the only thing baffling about Aunt Bell. Even as a small child, I felt her warmth, and I instinctively knew that Aunt Bell was very dear to my mother.

Little did I know that while Mark and I straddled Aunt Bell's propane tank pretending to ride horses and the chicken stewed in the pot, Aunt Bell and my mother extended a long tradition of sharing stories. Without Aunt Bell, my mother would have known nothing about the first weeks of her mother Mildred's life. Mildred never discussed her birth mother Lula with Irma or any of her children, nor did she share with them that her husband, Heber, was not a good man.

But Aunt Bell, the original family storyteller, had no problem discussing Lula and Heber with her niece, Irma (my mother). "I was mesmerized by Aunt Bell's stories. I would sit for hours and listen to her," my mother told me. My mother gained my full attention when she shared one of her conversations with Aunt Bell, and I, too, sat mesmerized by what she said:

"But I do say this: What my Aunt Bell told me about Grandma Lou had to be true. Aunt Bell had a memory. She's not like me. She could remember ten times more than I could. And she thought my grandma was the scum of the earth.

"Aunt Bell was an essential link in the chain of my childhood. She was loving and kind, and she always loved Mama. I guess Aunt Bell and Aunt Nin loved Mama more than they loved Aunt Izy and Uncle Lee.

"The only thing I remember Aunt Bell said about my Daddy is that he was not a good man for Mom. Aunt Bell told me what I could handle at my age. She said we'd talk about it when I was a mother and when I got married. She said she would tell me what a hard time my mother had, how Daddy was, and how he pursued her.

"Mama was leaving Daddy all the time, going back to Aunt Bell and

Aunt Nin because they had the means to take care of her. He was mean to her, but Mama was always taken good care of by Aunt Nin and Aunt Bell, and they were in a position to help her."

Irma's mother, Mildred May Poppell, was only seventeen years old on January 18, 1923, when she dropped her middle name and left her childhood home to become Mrs. Mildred P. Robinson. Mildred soon learned that living with her new husband and his parents on the Robinson farm was nothing like living with her loving, supportive Poppell family and never would be.

Five years older than Mildred, Heber Robinson was controlling, manipulative, cruel, and hot-headed. He shared no traits with her kind, gentle adoptive father, the only man she knew before Heber. Mildred had never seen a violent man before; Heber frightened her. She wanted to go home, back to her sisters Nina and Bell. She longed for her old life and the comfort and security she knew with the Poppells. Poor Mildred attempted to divorce Heber two times, but Heber always outsmarted her and stopped the divorce proceedings. I was all ears when my mother talked about her parents, Heber and Mildred:

"When Mom was married, you had to have three decrees when you got a divorce. And I don't know how much time in between those decrees there was. She left him when Norma was a baby. And right before that last decree was final, he lured her. He must have had a car, and he lured her and drove her around in Odum so people could see them. And Aunt Bell said that if people getting a divorce were seen together, the divorce was void. He did the same when I was a baby. He was mean to her."

Nina and Bell were powerless against Heber's dominance over their sister. So, they did what they could to help Mildred and her baby daughters, who were not only living with a brutal man but were also living with very little money. Heber rarely had a job, and when he did, he spent most of his paycheck on himself.

Mildred and her daughters, Norma and Irma, were always welcomed into Nina's and Bell's open arms and out of Heber's. And although the respites were short and always ended with Heber promising to be a better husband and convincing Mildred to return home, they were packed with good times and the familiarity of the Poppell home that Mildred missed terribly.

When Norma and Irma arrived at Aunt Nin and Aunt Bell's house, their aunts presented them with new shoes, socks, undergarments, and beautiful handmade dresses. And there was always good food for them to eat and, of course, lots of hugs and kisses.

Many times, Nina and Bell loaded Mildred and the girls in Nina's car for a short trip to Waycross to see their brother Lee. Mildred, Norma, and Irma would have felt a million miles away from their life back home with Heber when they were with Aunt Nin and Aunt Bell.

One of the few photographs I have of my mother as a child documents the early years she and Norma spent with their aunts Nin and Bell. In the photo, my mother and Norma are standing side by side in ribbon and lace embellished dresses sewn by Nina and Bell, wearing shiny black patent leather shoes and white socks that Nina had purchased for them. My mother is about three years old; Norma is about six in the photograph taken by Aunt Nin.

The girls look sad, standing together, not smiling and not touching one another, their arms by their sides. Or maybe Norma and Irma weren't unhappy but scared of the camera, or perhaps Aunt Nin had just given strict orders to stand up straight and not move. Or maybe there was genuine sadness in their expressions because they sensed their mother's hopelessness and knew they were soon going back home to Heber.

Mildred's husband and father of her children, Heber Ashmore Robinson. They say the eyes are windows to the soul, and when I look into his, I see darkness.

CHAPTER 2

Trapped in the Whirlwind

WHEN I ASKED MY MOTHER if she knew how or when her mother met Heber, she emphatically replied, "No, I do not, I do not. My mother was a very private person, and we never talked about that." Since my mother never discussed Heber with me either, I learned of his existence when my teenage brother Jody, my younger brother Mark, and I cruised through our hometown, Jesup, Georgia.

I was five or six years old; Mark was three or four, and we loved our drives to the Dairy Queen for a cherry Coke with our big brother and, as luck would have it, down *Cherry* Street. But our luck ran out the day Jody pointed out a creepy old man with unkempt hair and wrinkled clothes sitting on a bench and announced, "That's your grandpa."

"No, he is not!" I protested. Having never seen Heber before or known he existed, I was horrified to think the bum on the street was my grandpa. I remember pleading with Jody to tell me he was only kidding, but he never did. He never did because, sadly, what Jody told me was true. That dirty old man was my grandpa, and I was afraid of him.

Heber lived in a dusty, dark room in a fleabag hotel across the street from the teenage pool hall, near the bus station and train depot in Jesup. Pool halls must have been trendy in the early '60s in small-town America; Jesup retained two of them, one for adults and one for teenagers eighteen and under. One day while playing pool in the teenage pool hall, sixteen-year-old Jody heard a male voice declare, "I know who you are, and I bet you know who I am."

"No—I don't know who you are." But Jody did know who Heber was, and he had heard enough about him to conclude he wanted nothing to do with him.

And that was the way it was with Heber; no one wanted anything to do with him in his final years as he slowly disappeared into a world of alcohol, maladies, mental confusion, and isolation. Indigent, ill, and with no family willing to care for him, Heber checked into Central State Hospital in Milledgeville, Georgia, in his late sixties. While Heber was a patient at Central State in the 1960s, the hospital provided state-funded psychological and physical care for Georgia's destitute and needy citizens. It had long given up its practice of labeling mentally ill patients "lunatics" when Heber was a patient.

Central State Hospital, founded in 1842 as the Georgia Lunatic Asylum, grew into the largest mental institution in the world. Today the uninhabited hospital buildings still stand with historical markers identifying them. I recently toured the outside of the female convalescent building, now the Cornerstone/Auditorium Building on the old hospital property, and discovered these words inscribed on a historic plaque in front of it:

> The Georgia Lunatic Asylum (Now Central State Hospital) "was the fifth oldest institution exclusively for the insane in the South and the fourteenth in the nation"—Dr. Peter G. Cranford. It took care of the afflicted paupers in Georgia as well as others from Georgia and elsewhere who could pay $100/year to cover clothing, room and board, and medical care. The female convalescent building was erected in 1883. The back portion of the building once mirrored the Walker Building, the building directly across the Pecan Grove from this building. The back portion of the building was torn

down and a modern auditorium erected in 1949. The front portion was saved because it has a cornerstone with the hospital's original name of the Georgia Lunatic Asylum. The auditorium is still used for dances, meetings, nursing school graduations, and staff training and can also be rented for community events.

Examples of why you would be admitted to the hospital:

- 22-year-old white female; a pay patient who had been mentally ill for 8 years; indecent and immodest; ulcerated legs and other somewhat minor complaints; some improvement
- 23-year-old female; "lunatic and epileptic" whose epileptic convulsions seemed to follow disappointment in love; violent; hostile; auditory and visual hallucinations

In 1997, the Georgia Consumer Council began a restoration project at Central State Hospital's Cedar Lane Cemetery and built a memorial to the 25,000 souls buried there. Volunteers retrieved only two thousand of the mowed-over and weed-covered metal stakes that once marked each grave with only a number. Today the stakes are neatly arranged in the ground among a backdrop of a life-size bronze angel in honor of the forgotten, nameless patients heartlessly thrown into shallow graves.

Heber is not in Cedar Lane Cemetery. Someone in his Robinson family retrieved his body from Milledgeville and buried him in the Piney Grove Cemetery in Odum, Georgia, where my mother took me before she passed away. Heber's parents, Monroe and Maggie Robinson, and his brothers Claude and Ralph, are buried there.

Upon noticing the absence of Heber's gravesite among the other Robinsons, my mother read my mind and the expression on my face and said, "He's way over there."

That is where he belonged…way over there, I thought. Heber had not earned the respect of a burial near his family.

As we approached his gravesite, I asked my mother to give me her cane; with a baffled look on her face, she passed it to me. Little did she know I would use it to strike the concrete slab over Heber's body. And as I remember, Mother whacked it a few times too.

Heber Ashmore Robinson was born January 1, 1901, in Madray Springs, Georgia, a small farming community not far from Odum to Monroe and Maggie Robinson. He was one of six boys and four girls, number eight of ten. The Robinson boys were all quite handsome, especially Heber; the Robinson girls were also nice-looking.

Gertrude, one of the Robinson girls, received all the attention because of her flamboyant style and outgoing personality. When Jody was a little boy, Gertrude, dressed in elegant, colorful clothes, visited our mother. Having never seen any lady in heavy makeup adorned with necklaces, earrings, and bracelets and wearing feathers and jewels in her hat, he asked our mother, "Is she a queen?"

Gertrude, the "queen," and Heber's other siblings, married and moved out of their home with Monroe and Maggie, all except Heber and his brother Ralph. In 1923, when twenty-two-year-old Heber married seventeen-year-old Mildred May Poppell and moved her into his parents' home, Monroe and Maggie were delighted to welcome another daughter-in-law to live with them temporarily. But unlike Ralph, who moved out when his first child was born, Heber was in no hurry to vacate after having his first child or his second one either.

Heber was twenty-nine years old and worked as a truck driver for naval stores, the turpentine industry, in 1930. He had an income to provide a modest home for his twenty-four-year-old wife, Mildred, and his daughters, two-year-old Irma and five-year-old Norma. But instead, he chose to live with his parents and spend his paltry earnings on himself while Nina and Bell took care of his wife and daughters.

After nine years, it was time for Heber to go. Monroe's and Maggie's patience with their son, whose family had grown from two children to three when a third daughter, Frankie, was born, must have been tested to the breaking point. When Heber's older brother Brinson suggested that Heber's family live with him until they could find their own house, Heber, the moocher, accepted Brinson's offer. But again, Heber overstayed his welcome, and Brinson put Heber out too.

Luckily, when Brinson kicked Heber out of his house, Monroe deeded plots of lands on his farm to each of his children. A little shanty house built by Heber but never finished soon appeared on Heber's fifty-two acres. Heber did not paint the house or install plumbing, electricity, or windows; the shanty's wooden shutters were the only barrier from cold wind gusts. Without interior doors or walls, only exposed studs, the house provided no privacy for Heber's family.

During the early years living in the shanty house, Irma and her older sister Norma bought groceries every two weeks, paying for them on a run account. The rice, sugar, eggs, and flour they carried up the hill from Jimmy Poppell's grocery store kept the family fed. My mother swore they would have starved to death without Grandpa Monroe's vegetable garden after Jimmy closed the run account and refused to give Irma and Norma any more groceries until Heber paid up. Irma and Norma were minor children when they shopped for the family's food and worked on the farm. Buying groceries and milking the cows were their easiest chores; growing corn was much harder.

While Heber lounged on the porch reading, his daughters, Irma and Norma, toiled behind Uncle Ralph's mule and plow day after day until all three acres of the garden were ready for planting. While the tired, old mule rested, the girls dropped corn seeds into the freshly turned earth one by one. As their small hands covered each kernel, a feeling of dread overwhelmed Norma and Irma… Soon, they would have to pick the ears, feed some of them to the cows, and deliver the rest to the mill for grinding into grits and meal.

With nothing to do since his children did all the work on the farm, after a few years, Heber grew bored and decided to lease his house and land. With rent money in his pocket, Heber moved Mildred, Norma, Irma, and Frankie out of the farmhouse into a rental house at the Crossroads in Jesup, a small community near Madray Springs where several roads "cross."

The Crossroads House was much more suitable for a growing family than the shack on the farm; Irma fondly recalled that it had low ceilings, finished walls rather than exposed studs, bedroom doors, a kitchen, and a living room. Irma did not want to leave the Crossroads, but after about three years, the renters left the shanty house, and Heber moved Mildred, Irma, Frankie, and the new baby, Puddin, back into it.

Like many families in Madray Springs, Heber's family was poor and had little money for extras, not even clothing. But Mildred and her daughters always wore presentable clothes Heber's sisters "handed down" to them. Irma remembered gleefully tearing through bags of hand-me-down dresses Heber's sisters Gertrude and Ira and their daughters either outgrew or grew tired of wearing. And of course, Aunt Bell continued sewing for her nieces, and as they grew older, the girls selected the dress styles they liked in the Sears catalog for her to copy. Irma never wore pants until she turned fifteen and started her first job.

Irma recollected that several of her friends' families received either government commodities or a check for service in WWI. But because Heber owned his farm and did not serve in WWI, he did not qualify for government assistance.

Irma's best friend Wilma's father was a WWI veteran and, under the Bonus Act of 1924, was awarded additional pay after his service. Veterans were given $1 for every day of service in the United States and $1.25 per day for service outside of the United States paid as bonuses spread out over twenty years to limit government spending. The bonus payments Wilma's father received provided extra money for her family to purchase the most delicious treat Irma had ever eaten.

One day while at Wilma's, Irma spied some peanut butter in the cupboard and asked if she could taste it. With the jar in one hand and a spoon in the other, Irma dipped into the gooey goodness, licked the spoon clean, and vowed that if she ever had any money, she would buy a jar of peanut butter for herself.

Irma never forgot how good that golden goo tasted; when she was fifteen and had a job, she secretly purchased a jar of it and consumed it all in an hour. Irma soon realized that gulping down more than a spoonful or two of peanut butter was not a good idea and became very ill. Afraid to admit what she had done, Irma tossed the empty jar and pretended that the food she ate at school made her sick. The experience did not negatively affect my mother because peanut butter was always in our cabinets, although my father usually ate most of it.

Irma's only pleasant memories of her childhood involved her friend Wilma and Irma's grandparents, Maggie and Monroe Robinson. Irma's first cousin, Dorothy DuBreuil, eloquently captured her memories of her grandparents, Maggie and Monroe, in these poems:

Gone are the days of summertime, of feeding the chicks on the farm,
pulling the water up from the well and hiding in Grandpa's barn.
Gone is the house we used to love, gone is the old fig tree,
gone is that feeling so special to us when young and so free.
I still see "FatMa's" white apron as she wiped her tears away,
the wave of her hand as we left her to go each on our separate way.
—Excerpts from "Ode to the Robinsons"
by Dorothy Nell Ogden DuBreuil

Thanks for dear Grand Papa out in his old canoe with grandkids, not a few. He'd overturn the darned old thing and scare it out of you. Oh my! What a lark! These are the memories we're after, of all the good scares and the laughter. And did we all shake every rafter, and Grandma's ghosts we loved the most. Thanks for the memories of peaches sweet and yellow, of watermelons mellow, of butter beans and collard greens, and cornbread for each fellow. We all ate our fill. Thanks for the memories of chicken

that Grandma fried, that Grandpa killed with pride. We ate it with big biscuits and slopped gravy on the side. We thank them so much.
—Excerpts from "Thanks for the Memory"
by Dorothy Nell Ogden DuBreuil

Irma and Dorothy shared lots of good times with their grandparents and always spoke fondly of them. Irma adored her grandpa, Monroe, naming her fourth child Mark Monroe after him. Grandpa Monroe loved his children and grandchildren very much, and everyone loved him. He was nothing like his wicked son Heber.

If only Grandpa Monroe knew that Heber transformed into a monster when Mildred and the children moved out of his house. If only he knew that Heber beat Norma and Irma, Grandpa Monroe could have interceded and spared them from Heber's leather strap.

But he was unaware that Heber abused his daughters, and both girls had no other choice but to flee their country home in Madray Springs when they were teenagers. Norma was the first to go.

Mildred's first child, Norma, about thirty-six years old, playfully posing on one of her many automobiles. Circa 1960.

CHAPTER 3

Into the Winds of Freedom

LIKE MANY INEXPERIENCED GIRLS, Heber and Mildred's oldest daughter, Norma, dreamed of a knight in shining armor coming to take her far away from her miserable life. When she met and married "Tuff" Strickland, she believed her knight had finally come for her even though he wore overalls. Tuff was no knight and had no shining armor, but he did whisk her away and moved her into town in Jesup. Norma was only fifteen years old when they married, and it didn't take Mrs. Norma Strickland long to realize that marrying anyone named Tuff was a mistake and that she was again living with an abusive man.

My older sister Sandra remembers meeting Tuff when she was about seven years old and noticing a large protrusion growing on his forehead. Sandra wasn't sure what it was, but to her, it looked like what she had seen on each side of a cow's head, and she decided to call him "Horn."

Sandra did not recall Norma's husband's real name when she became an adult; she remembered only the name she gave him and insisted that it was Horn, not Tuff. Since our mother had not noticed the growth on Tuff's head, she argued with Sandra that she must be confused. Unable to convince her daughter that Norma's first husband's name was Tuff and not Horn, our mother abruptly ended the disagreement when she declared, "Norma was never married to a man with a horn on his head!"

After breaking free from the "horned" man, Norma still believed that her knight in shining armor was out there somewhere, and he would find her. And it wasn't long before her dream of a knight coming to save her came true when she met and married Jay Eason.

Mark and I remember sharing meals with Aunt Norma and Uncle Jay as children. Mark says Norma and Jay's house smelled like greasy food; I don't recall that. But we both remember that Norma was fun to be around and greeted our mother and us with big hugs each time we arrived at her home.

I thought that Aunt Norma and Uncle Jay looked a lot like photos I had seen of the "Fat Lady" and the "Thin Man" of the Ringling Bros. and Barnum & Bailey Circus. Like John Battersby (the Thin Man) and his wife Hannah (the Fat Lady), Jay was thin and Norma was plump and an odd pairing obvious even to a little child. But what wasn't strange about Aunt Norma and Uncle Jay was their admiration for one another and their happiness.

I have an old photograph of Jay, Aunt Bell, and Norma's dog. Norma inscribed on the back of it these words: "My sweet Aunt Bell and my husband, Jay, and my little dog, Minsey. I love them all very much. 'God bless them all' is my daily prayer."

Norma never forgot the affection and kindness shown to her by Aunt Bell when she was a child. According to my mother, after Norma married, she "slipped Aunt Bell a dollar here and a dollar there." Norma often went to Bell's house, taking her little sisters, Puddin and Melissy. Whenever Norma popped up at the girls' home in her Ford two-door ranch wagon, Puddin and Melissy eagerly jumped in, ready for adventures with the merrymaker in the family.

When the girls were twelve and fourteen, the movie *Singin' in the Rain* was showing at the Strand Theater in Jesup, and they dreamed of sitting in front of the big screen watching Gene Kelly and Debbie Reynolds sing and dance to the songs they had heard on the radio. If Norma had not given each of the girls a nickel for admission, it is unlikely that seeing the movie would have been anything but a dream for Puddin and Melissy. As it turned out, I am the one with the dream. I must have been intrigued with Puddin and Melissy's memories of

Norma and the day they watched *Singin' in the Rain* when I dreamed this:

One Saturday morning in 1952, Norma showed up at the girls' home for one of their day trips to Aunt Bell's house in the country. No longer interested in Bell's well, Puddin and Melissy pleaded with Norma to take them to the Strand Theater in Jesup to see *Singin' in the Rain* instead of driving to Aunt Bell's. When Norma explained that going to the movies was not a good idea, the girls were determined to change her mind.

Hearing the familiar *honk, honk* of Norma's wagon, the sisters gleefully fell into the back seat ready for a day of fun. As Norma's car rolled away, the girls sang out the words to one of Debbie Reynolds's songs in the movie, "Good morning, good morning, we've talked the whole night through. Good morning, good morning, to you!"

Norma's sisters knew some of the songs from the movie and serenaded Norma with them over and over during the drive to Aunt Bell's house. While at Aunt Bell's, the girls performed Gene Kelly's number, "Singin' in the Rain," as they twirled and skipped with the tattered and torn umbrella retrieved from Norma's car. Feeling a little manipulated but amused, Norma shortened her visit with Aunt Bell and dropped off her talented sisters at the Strand Theater on the way home.

When I shared my dreamed up *Singin' in the Rain* story with Puddin and Melissy, we all had a big laugh and agreed it was much better than the real one.

Puddin and Melissy have never forgotten the enjoyable times they spent going to church, riding out to the country to Aunt Bell's house, and going to the movies with their oldest sister. Norma never had much money or a grand home, but she shared what she had with those she loved. She could not have known that the coins she placed in her little sisters' hands purchased more than movie tickets; they paid for Puddin and Melissy to spend a few precious hours escaping from their misfortunate lives. Memories of the Strand Theater and their sister Norma have never left Puddin and Melissy's minds.

Norma's shining light burned out way too soon when she succumbed to diabetes at fifty-seven years old, two years after losing her beloved Jay. But her legacy lives today. She will always be the first of Heber and Mildred Robinson's children to escape into the winds of freedom. My mother, Irma, soon followed.

Mildred's second child, Irma Gail, proudly presenting her firstborn in 1946.

CHAPTER 4

The Gail Force Wind

NORMA LEFT TWELVE-YEAR-OLD Irma behind on the farm when she married Tuff. With Norma absent from the home, Irma became the oldest child and the only one with daily chores in the Heber Robinson family. Frankie and Puddin were seven and one when Norma married and not old enough to do the work their father should have done; it all fell on Irma.

Even though Heber imposed upon his daughter hard labor, Irma excelled in school, walking to the elementary school in Madray Springs until the seventh grade, when she began riding the bus to the nearby Piney Grove School. After school each day, Mr. Ogden, the bus driver, dropped Irma off at a neighbor's house; Irma could see her house in the field from the Delks' house—no grass, just a swept yard.

The house with the swept yard held painful memories for Irma, ones that she shared only with my older brother Jody's wife, Nancy:

"Frannie Miller, Heber's aunt, was staying with us. While she was there, one night, Heber came home drunk, and Mama told him that I didn't mind her. He yelled and cussed at me and then beat me. And this time, he pointed a long gun at me and threatened to shoot me.

"Frannie told me to go to Grandpa Monroe, so I ran through the fields and made it to Uncle Claude's house. I was soaked in sweat and tears when Uncle Claude asked, 'What in the hell are you doing out here this time of night?' I told him that Heber nearly beat me to death, and he pulled a gun on me. Uncle Claude said, 'Don't tell Pa. He'll kill the son of a bitch!'

"Emmaline and Holland Madray, Uncle Claude and Aunt Mildred's friends, were having dinner with them that night and they took me back home, assuming that Heber would be sleeping off the alcohol.

"Uncle Claude contacted Doug Thomas, a prestigious lawyer and former schoolmate of my mother's, about the incident. I wanted to leave home, but Mr. Thomas said to wait, and I could always leave later."

About a year after the night Heber pulled a gun on Irma, she turned fifteen on May 19, 1942, without any fanfare. Instead of giving his daughter a birthday cake or a gift, Heber declared that Irma was old enough to have a job and would not return to school for her tenth year.

That same year the United States was embroiled in World War II, and Heber learned that the shipyards in Brunswick, Georgia, forty miles from Jesup, were hiring welders to assemble ships for the war effort. Brunswick, Georgia, was one of sixteen ports chosen to construct cargo vessels called "Liberty Ships" to transport supplies to the Allied forces in Europe. With the declaration of war by the United States, the shipyard laborers constructed each Liberty Ship with incredible speed in about three months. Sixteen thousand workers built ninety-nine Liberty Ships from 1941 to 1945. My teenage mother was one of those workers for a short time.

Obeying Heber's order to provide income for the family, fifteen-year-old Irma carpooled from Madray Springs to Jesup and caught the Maritime Commission bus to the Brunswick shipyard for an interview with Mr. Mixon in the summer of 1942. Heber was aware that the high-paying welder position required sixteen years and older applicants, so he instructed Irma to lie about her age. Heber's strategy worked; Mr. Mixon did not question Irma's age of "sixteen" and hired her as a welder on the spot.

During one of my mother's interviews with Nancy, she shared this memory of her employment at the shipyard. But like most stories that involve Heber, it has a tragic ending:

"Another girl and I welded the bottoms of new boats in the fabrication shop. We wore hard hats and coveralls and climbed like a couple of monkeys. We weren't afraid of the heights or the vertical welding work. I developed a reputation as being a hard and dependable worker. I made good money, and I turned it over to Heber every week.

"After about six months on the job, I decided to buy leather coats for Frankie and me. I kept enough money from my pay for the jackets and turned over the remaining salary to Heber. He was furious that I did not give all my earnings to him so he beat me with a leather strap. I can still hear him yelling, 'If you can't give me your check, you won't work!'"

After Heber's last lash Irma raised her trembling body off the floor, took a deep breath, and thought: *I'm running for my life and this time I'm not coming back.* When Heber turned away from her, Irma bolted for the door and fled through the darkness, running along the stream that led to Uncle Ralph and Aunt Pearl's house.

Heber followed close behind in a drunken pursuit, never coming close enough to catch Irma. But he was close enough to hear a defiant, brave young girl proclaim, "You will never beat me again!" as Uncle Ralph pulled his battered and traumatized niece into the safety of his home.

Irma trusted Uncle Ralph and knew he would help her, so when he summoned Sheriff Robert Warren, Irma felt safe from Heber. Irma was only fifteen years old when she pulled down the top of her coveralls, worn that day while welding, to show Sheriff Warren what Heber did to her. Seeing the strap marks and wounds on Irma's flesh, Sheriff Warren gasped in disbelief. "I wouldn't beat a mule of mine like that, much less a child."

Irma heard Sheriff Warren tell her Uncle Ralph that if Heber did not obey his orders to leave, he would arrest him, but Irma feared that if Heber left, he would soon return. She remembered what her mother's friend, the lawyer, had said to her the last time Heber hurt her: *You can always leave later.* For Irma, it was "later," and there was no way she was ever going back home to Heber.

The next day Ralph escorted Irma home to pack her clothes and tell her mother she had made arrangements to move in with Norma and Tuff. Irma's heart ripped apart as she kissed Frankie, Puddin, and her baby sister, Melissy, and promised she would come back for them someday.

Frankie was the hardest one for Irma to leave. She and Frankie had always been close; their separation was traumatic for them. Irma had insulated Frankie from Heber's beatings and had been a mother figure to her. Ironically, Irma's selfless, motherly act of buying ten-year-old Frankie a new coat separated the two sisters.

Broken-hearted but determined to save herself, Irma walked to her old bus stop to wait for Norma after retrieving her belongings. Her new leather coat, zipped up tightly, warmed her purple-and-black-striped back, and she wore it proudly as a trophy earned for defying Heber's tyranny. Her view clouded by tears she tried to suppress, Irma recognized her old bus driver, Mr. Ogden, coming down the road.

Surprised to see Irma standing at the bus stop, Mr. Ogden pulled over and asked why she wasn't at work. When Irma embarrassingly disclosed that Heber had beat her badly and she had run away from home, Mr. Ogden suggested that she live with his wife and him. Irma graciously declined and told Mr. Ogden she was going to live with Norma in Jesup.

Getting Irma fired was Heber's coup de gras. If he couldn't have Irma's pay, he ensured that she wouldn't have it either. But Heber did not anticipate Mr. Mixon's offer of a position in the gas ration office, where Irma was old enough to work. Of course, Irma accepted the job, but her employment in the office did not last long. After only two days, Mildred begged Irma to come back home. Reluctantly, Irma quit her office job and agreed to help her mother with her siblings for only a few days. She did not trust Sheriff Warren to arrest Heber if he returned.

When I learned that my mother ran away from home when she was only fifteen years old, I realized she was the strongest, bravest person I knew. I was in awe of her. One user of the Urban Dictionary named LovelyLinda defined "Irma" in her December 30, 2014 post as a beautiful, strong, independent warrior who "always fights for freedom…" Irma

Robinson was born beautiful, strong, independent, and a warrior who fought hard for and won her freedom.

When fifteen-year-old Irma freed herself from Heber, she had no middle name—the one thing Heber and Mildred could have given her that was free. With her newfound independence, Irma Robinson proclaimed that her full name was Irma "Gail" Robinson and began a new life living with Norma.

I don't know if my mother ever realized the significance of the name she chose for herself and then gave to me. But I appreciated its meaning when I began describing her as a "Gail" Force Wind in homage to her strength and ultimate dominance over her abusive father. I am honored that my mother named me Angela Gail, and I am proud that three more "Gail Force Winds" followed me: my daughter, Stephanie Gail; my best friend Molly's daughter, Olivia Gail; and the fourth generation "Gail Force Wind," my sister's granddaughter, Sienna Gail.

Irma's journey to a better life free from hardship and suffering was long and arduous, but with "Gail" force winds propelling her, she was unstoppable, doing whatever she had to do to survive, never pitying herself.

There was no time for school while Irma lived with Norma and Tuff; instead, she worked Monday through Friday, walking two miles to the shirt factory in Jesup to press shirts and earn rent money to pay Tuff. Irma pumped water from a well every Saturday, boiled it in a large wash pot filled with lye, and scrubbed and rinsed Norma's dresses and Tuff's overalls in it three times.

It wasn't long before Irma made an astute observation that there had to be a better job for her other than washing and ironing clothes, so she applied for a nurse's aide position at the Colvin-Ritch-Leapheart Hospital in Jesup. Dr. Ritch, the hospital director, hired Irma and approved her admittance into the nurses' dormitory the summer she turned sixteen in 1943. Irma's nurse's aide job awarded her a place to live, free meals, and a salary of $1.50 a week that increased to five dollars a week after a year. Irma's recollections of working at the hospital and attending school:

"When school started back in the fall, Dr. Ritch urged me to go back and begin my tenth year. I told him that I couldn't go back to school and that I had to support myself. I had no intention of going to school for my tenth-grade year, but Dr. Ritch insisted that I go.

"He talked about my situation with Mrs. Virginia Coleman, the superintendent of nurses. She agreed to allow me to work afternoons and every other weekend since I had been doing such an excellent job with the patients.

"To be at school on time and get the maximum amount of sleep, I skipped breakfast at the hospital most days, and since I had very little money, I usually skipped lunch at school. After school and my 4:00-to-6:30 shift, I ate dinner. Lots of times, the hospital cooks sneaked extra food to me."

In March 1945, after working as a nurse's aide for nearly two years, seventeen-year-old Irma reported wearing a freshly starched nursing uniform and white polished nursing shoes for her after-school shift. One of her duties as a nurse's aide was to bring newborns from the nursery to their mother's hospital rooms.

The day Irma presented Harrell Hodge to his anxiously awaiting parents, she caught the eye of a very handsome young man in the room more interested in her than in his brother's new baby. While gazing upon the stunning young lady carrying his nephew, Joe Hodge thought: *I saw it, I liked it, and I'm gonna have it.*

Soon after baby boy Hodge checked out, big boy Hodge "checked in." Joe Hodge was spotted numerous times cruising by the hospital in his 1941 Dodge hoping to get a glimpse of the captivating young woman he intently watched cradle Harrell in her slender arms.

Not long after their chance encounter, Irma began waving to Joe from the upper balcony of the hospital as he drove by, and after months of wooing her, Joe's persistence paid off. Irma ended her relationship with another suitor and accepted Joe's marriage proposal.

Irma was attracted to Joe because of his cleanliness and neat clothing. She remembers that he wore laundered white shirts, ties, and khaki pants and that he had a career and a car. Joe's parents equally impressed Irma, who realized she was marrying into a much better family than hers.

Joe's father, David Martin Hodge, was a successful farmer and mule trader living in Screven, Georgia, a small town near Jesup. "D. M." Hodge devoted himself to supporting and caring for his wife and children, and although he was not a kind father, he never deserted his children like Heber deserted his. Joe's mother, Mattie, was a schoolteacher and nothing like Irma's uneducated and unsophisticated mother.

Irma was confident Joe was a good man from a good family and wanted to marry him, but she needed Grandpa Monroe's blessing and approval. Irma never forgot the day Joe met Grandpa Monroe on the farm: "My grandpa was one of the most beloved citizens of Wayne County and I respected his opinion. When he said, 'Irmie, you've picked the right man,' I knew Joe was the one for me."

After Irma married Joe, Irma struggled with whether she should continue attending school and working at the hospital:

"I wanted to quit school, be a wife, and just work. My teacher, Mr. Lemuel Paul, tried to persuade me to return to class after Christmas, but there was no way I was going back. I had Joe, and I wasn't interested in school anymore or working at the hospital.

"I worked at the hospital only one more month after quitting school. I could not continue going to school or work because I was pregnant with Jody and had severe nausea. I already had a class ring and a graduation gown that I paid for with money Mrs. Dale Smith, the hospital bookkeeper, loaned me.

"I turned in my books and buried that class ring in Joe's brother-in-law Hubert's garden, only five months away from graduation. I was indebted to Dr. Ritch for all he did for me. He always told me that there would be a scholarship for me to go to nursing school when I graduated high school. But I can honestly say I never regretted not finishing school. Dr. Ritch was disappointed when I got married, but I was so in love with Joe. I had no role model to encourage me to wait to get married."

Irma married Joe Hodge on November 2, 1945, at the home of her friend Sara Howard, whose father was a justice of the peace. Joe was nineteen; Irma was eighteen. Their wedding announcement appeared in the local newspaper:

> Robinson-Hodge
>
> A quiet ceremony was performed Friday night, November 2, at the home of D.S. Howard, Justice of the Peace, in Ludowici, uniting a very popular young couple, Irma Robinson, daughter of Mr. and Mrs. H.A. Robinson of Jesup, and Joe Hodge, son of Mr. and Mrs. D.M. Hodge of Screven. Those present were Beatrice Ensley, Sara Howard, Margaret Reddish, Warren Robinson and Mrs. D.S. Howard. The bride was attired in a lovely suit of blue with black accessories. A beautiful corsage completed her ensemble.
>
> Mrs. Hodge had been connected with Colvin-Ritch Hospital for the past two years. Mr. Hodge had been connected with the McCann Lumber Company at Doctortown for the past two and a half years. After a short wedding trip to Savannah, the couple are making their home, temporarily on Brunswick Street in Jesup.
>
> (*The Jesup Sentinel*, 1945)

After their honeymoon in Savannah, Irma and Joe moved into a temporary home until they settled in Doctortown, a thriving sawmill and lumber community located a few miles north of Jesup on the banks of the Altamaha River.

White settlers chose the name Doctortown when they opened a post office in 1857 on land once inhabited by Native Americans and a medicine man named Alleck, the Muskogean Indian word meaning doctor.

Destiny dictated that Irma and Joe would live in a place called Doctortown; after all, they met in a hospital.

Joe began working in Doctortown in 1943 for the McCann Lumber Company when he was seventeen years old and continued working there for twenty years. Joe maintains the only reason the lumber company hired him to work in their office is that he had no problem assuming a clerical position typically filled by women.

Joe's agreeable disposition coincidentally landed him a chair in his high school concert band as the cello player. Because the girls refused to place a cello between their knees while wearing skirts and none of the boys would play it, Joe volunteered.

But Joe soon became bored with the instrument the other band members would not play, so he entertained himself by sneaking in unrehearsed extra notes during the band's performances. Recognizing Joe's musical talent and his cleverness, the director allowed Joe to play the cello in his unique style, and the Joe Hodge lick was born.

As a child, I remember waking in a huff on Saturday and Sunday mornings to my dad banging out gospel tunes on the piano, always incorporating his signature lick. His strumming of Hank Williams's songs on his guitar in the evenings while my siblings and I strained to hear the television was equally annoying. But we realize now that having music echoing through our home and planted in our DNA was a blessing.

More than fifty years passed before the musical seeds in Joe's children sprouted, and they began singing and playing music. The oldest child, Jody, plays the harmonica; the fourth child, Mark, plays the piano, guitar, and banjo; and I play the autoharp and dobro. The second child, Sandra, writes song lyrics and says she plays the didgeridoo, although we cannot find a place for it in the band. Together we are the "Monroe Pickers," a name we chose to honor our mother's Grandpa Monroe and her fourth child, Mark Monroe. Our dad would have been amazed at our "back porch picking" during family gatherings, and he would be incredibly proud of his first great-grandchild, Leah, a masterful cello player!

The intrepid teenager who had no problem playing the cello when no one else would, became the leading candidate for the McCann Lumber Company's secretarial position in Doctortown. Because the company office had no bathroom and the male staff's crude language disrespected women, the McCann Lumber Company employed only men in their office. Since Joe could type, take shorthand, and keep books, all rare skills possessed by men at that time, he landed his first job. Two years later he married my mother and moved her into one of the company-owned mill houses.

An active narrow trestle bridge built in 1914 still stands over the Altamaha River in Doctortown. Joe and Irma would have heard and seen countless numbers of trains pass over the bridge during their eight years in Doctortown. But they could have never imagined the tragedy that would occur more than sixty years later when Sarah Jones lost her life on it in 2014.

Sarah Jones was a camera assistant for the movie *Midnight Rider*, a drama based on Gregg Allman's autobiography, *My Cross to Bear*. On February 20, 2014, the *Midnight Rider* movie crew assembled on the old trestle bridge to film a scene depicting its version of a dream described by Gregg Allman in this passage from *My Cross to Bear*:

I was sitting up talking, and I just kind of nodded off. But I didn't nod off; I was Code Blue. I was bleeding inside, and I was drowning in my own blood.

What I remember is that I went to sleep and I had the most incredible dream. It was almost a still life, and the air smelled so good and music was playing. I always have music in my dreams, and whatever type of music it is, it sets the whole mood for whatever's happening. If it's a nightmare, it's some nasty music. But this music was beautiful.

I was standing at a bridge and it was twilight, and somebody was on the other side. They weren't motioning, they were just looking at me, but the message got through: don't come across this bridge. It was all so beautiful; I wanted to go over there and see who it was. All I could see was a silhouette of the person, with hair down to their shoulders. It appeared to be my brother. Maybe it was just somebody standing in my room, I don't know. But somebody was there, telling me not to come across that bridge. It's not my time yet.

As the crew prepared to shoot the dream sequence in *Midnight Rider*, actor William Hurt, portraying Gregg, lay on a hospital bed placed on the trestle high above the Altamaha River while actor Wyatt Russell positioned himself on the tracks holding a guitar, acting as Duane. But instead of filming the movie scene, the camera operators captured the actors and crew members scrambling to get off the trestle only seconds before a CSX train traveling fifty-seven miles per hour with two locomotives and thirty-seven freight cars barreled over it and smashed into the hospital bed. Sarah Jones could not exit the trestle before the train entered it.

Seven other crew members were injured, one seriously. The district attorney's office in Wayne County, Georgia, charged three directors and producers with involuntary manslaughter in Sarah's death. OSHA cited them for "serious" and "willful" safety violations. Production of the movie ceased after Gregg joined others who called for its shutdown, and William Hurt refused to participate in any further filming.

It is impossible to view photos of that old trestle today without envisioning the day Sarah Jones lost her life on it. But for me, it will always be a bittersweet reminder of the years my parents lived in Doctortown and their humble beginnings in the little mill house.

While living in one of the rent-free mill houses in Doctortown, Irma had a home again, after fleeing hers at fifteen. My mother was proud to be Mrs. Joe Hodge. Her newfound chores would have seemed like child's play compared to her work at the shirt factory, and she overlooked the house's primitive furnishings. The old wood-burning stove did not intimidate her; she quickly learned to cook delicious meals on it. But after a couple of months, Irma didn't do much cooking; she was severely nauseated and pregnant with her first child, Joseph Jr., the honeymoon baby, the child Irma called "my Jody."

Jody lived the first seven years of his life in Doctortown, and after moving away, he returned often to fish along the banks of the Altamaha River and, when he was old enough, to assist his father in the office on weekends. Jody composed a written account of his childhood in Doctortown and shared it with me.

"The mill in Doctortown employed about five hundred direct employees and another 150 contracted employees such as independent loggers and truck drivers. Doctortown consisted of the mill and its various operations, a company store, a railway freight depot, a post office, a café, ten or fifteen mill houses for White families, and thirty or forty mill houses for Black families.

"Neither White nor Black families paid rent for their company houses. Most of the people who lived in the company houses did not have automobiles, so this close proximity to their work was important. The company housing areas were segregated, with the Black section being on one side of the railroad tracks and the White section on the other.

"Although I do not recall the denomination, there was a Black church in the Black section. I don't think there was a church for the White residents. There was no school in Doctortown, and the children living there rode the school bus to Jesup.

"I have many memories of the years we lived in Doctortown. Often on Sunday evenings, my dad drove the family to the Black church and parked outside, where we would sit in the car and listen to the congregation sing hymns.

"I have little memory of our first house, but by the time my sister was born, two years after me, we had moved to a larger home. I remember pretty well the second house because we lived there until I was seven. It was at the bend of the main and only road from Highway 301 to the mill. It had an outdoor privy, although my dad soon built an indoor bathroom, a small living room, a small kitchen, two pretty large bedrooms, and a Florida room. There was a porch on the front and one on the back of the house. The Florida room was accessed from the main bedroom and had windows on three sides. The windows could be opened in the summer to cool the room. My parents put a bed in this room, and I slept there during the summer months. I can remember standing in my baby bed and looking into this room at night and seeing the radio next to their bed glowing in the dark.

"My mother once told me that she doubted I could remember that since I was so young and most likely recalled pictures of the house rather than the house itself. However, our early pictures are black and white, and I think I convinced her that I remembered when I described my baby bed's color—red—and other items in the house.

"It seems everyone had dogs and puppies, and we had a milk cow in a shed behind our home. I don't think my dad or mother milked the cow, so I don't know why we had her. My dad tells me he had the cow to give us fresh milk and that he did milk her."

I've always liked hearing about those early years of my parents' marriage and the good ol' days in Doctortown. My mother found security and love in the little Doctortown house, and she put her painful past behind her. But she could not stop thinking about the mother and siblings she left behind when she ran away from home.

In 1947, only two years after Irma married, she received dreadful news. Heber sold the farmland and house in Madray Springs. Ignoring Irma's pregnant mother and four siblings while they moved from one dump to another was never an option for the "Gail Force Wind."

A few months after the Robinson family gathered for their only group photograph in 1947, Heber sold his home and farmland and dumped his family at Norma's house in town. *Back row, left to right:* Irma, age: 20; Frankie, age: 14; Mildred, age: 41; Heber, age 46; *front row:* Puddin, age: 8, and Melissy, age: 5. At the time of this photograph, Irma was married with a child, and Mildred was a few months pregnant with her last child.

CHAPTER 5
Lost in the Wind

A YEAR BEFORE HEBER SOLD the farm, Mildred begged him to spare her fourteen-year-old daughter from the same harsh work he forced on Norma and Irma, fearing that she, too, would run away. But Heber dismissed his wife's pleas, insisting that Frankie help him clear the undeveloped land on his property and prepare it for planting crops.

So, while Frankie attended school, unemployed, good-for-nothing Heber spent his days napping on the front porch until about thirty minutes before Frankie returned home. During those thirty minutes, Heber folded up his blankets to hide any evidence of his idleness, grabbed an ax and a machete, struck a tree a few times, and cut a bush or two.

Within moments of the bus arriving with Frankie, perspiration appeared on Heber's brow and clothes. Gasping for air and pretending to have been working all day, Heber bemoaned to Frankie and Mildred that he was too exhausted to continue, and Frankie must finish his work. Exchanging her schoolbooks for an ax, Frankie dutifully obeyed her father and chopped trees and cut back weeds and brush for hours each day after school.

After months of cleaning and dressing scrapes and wounds inflicted by the thorns in the brush on her daughter's frail body, Mildred found the courage to stand up to Heber and persuade him to stop working Frankie every day after school. Mildred could not have anticipated the price for freeing Frankie.

Without Frankie's help clearing the farmland and too lazy to do the work himself, Heber announced to Mildred and the children that he must sell their home and move into town with no land to clear and no fields and gardens to maintain. He did not tell his family that the real reason he sold the farm was to be with the woman he had been seeing in Jesup.

Heber sold out his family for fourteen hundred dollars, an amount equal to about twenty thousand dollars today, and abruptly dumped them at Norma and Jay's. At the same time, he and his girlfriend moved into the new house he bought with the proceeds from the sale of the farm.

Heber promised Norma that Mildred and the children would not be there for long, but history repeated itself, and Norma fell into the same trap Heber's father and brother fell into when Heber refused to leave. After an extended, uninvited stay, Norma and Jay insisted that Heber find another place for the family. So, Heber again displaced his wife and children.

Mildred's eleven-year-old great-granddaughter, Lori, Jody's daughter, interviewed Mildred in 1979 for a school project assigned to her by her teacher and mother, Nancy Hodge. Lori earned an "A" for her assignment and forever preserved Mildred's thoughts about Heber selling the farm and moving her and her children:

"After Heber sold the farm, we lived with Norma, and then we moved into a shack on the highway near Jesup. It wasn't fit to live in; it had no electricity or running water. Frankie and Puddin hauled water from another house. Irma was already married to Joe Hodge."

Frankie was fourteen years old when she and her siblings—Puddin, Melissy, and James—and her pregnant mother lost their home on the farm. Irma could not bear the thought of Heber displacing Frankie from the only home she had ever known and moving her from place to place like a gypsy as she entered high school.

With Joe's blessings, Irma kept the promise she made to Frankie to return for her someday when she moved her to Doctortown. Joe's heart dwarfed his bank account, yet he and Irma always managed to provide not only for their children but also for Irma's siblings. Frankie has never forgotten the hospitality Irma and Joe extended to her:

"I've always been a very grateful person. Just like I've always been so grateful for Irma and Joe. I often think and relive my life when I'm alone. And I think I not only ended up living with Irma and Joe, but Irma was also my idol growing up. And your mother and dad meant so much to me."

Frankie babysat Jody and cleaned the little mill house until she turned sixteen, and Irma arranged for her to live at the hospital in the nurse's housing and finish high school. Irma's own experience working there assured her that Dr. Ritch and his staff would take good care of her sister.

Frankie was eighty-eight years old when I asked her to recall living at the nurse's home while attending high school. Her memories of graduating, the outpouring of love and appreciation from her old friends in Jesup, and the new friends she made while working at the hospital have never left her:

"I lived at the hospital. They had a house they rented, and it was a nice house in a nice neighborhood. I lived there for free, and my meals were free at the hospital. So, you see, that was cash. People were so good to me. When I graduated, I got many gifts.

"Well, you know Jesup is a little town, and everybody was so proud of me for working and going to school. People would come to the hospital. I guess I was a pretty good nursing assistant and pretty well known, and people were always bringing me gifts. Of course, growing up, I had friends whose family had a dollar or two."

While Frankie lived with Irma and Joe and then at the nurse's home, Irma's sisters, Puddin and Melissy, remained displaced from their country home. They lived in deplorable conditions with their mother and baby brothers, James and Carl, while Heber shacked up in the house he bought for his girlfriend. Heber promised to bring them groceries every Saturday, but most Saturdays, he showed up drunk with no food, spending the grocery money on liquor instead. Heber was not an alcoholic; he did not have the luxury of drinking every day. He was a binge drinker, getting drunk when he had the money instead of buying food for his family.

Puddin remembers that green pea pies and vegetables cooked in lard were all she and her siblings had to eat most of the time. And she remembers her mother's pies tasted awful, and she usually went to school hungry, refusing to eat them.

Melissy remembers the day hunger overwhelmed Puddin's order not to eat at school unless Heber gave her money. She remembers standing in the free lunch line with her head down, thinking Puddin would not see her. As her stomach growled louder than Puddin's voice in her head telling her not to eat lunch without paying, six-year-old Melissy felt the familiar tug on her arm by Puddin. "You can't eat free lunches! You don't belong in this line with all the poor children. Everyone will know we are poor!" proclaimed Puddin as she pulled Melissy out of the free line.

Melissy never received a free meal that day or any other day, but she gained something much more valuable; she learned from her older sister never to allow her poverty-stricken life to define her. And she learned the importance of her dignity and pride.

Fortunately for the girls, they passed by Norma's house on the way home from school. Norma always had home cooked-meals on the stove or in the refrigerator and graciously shared them with her sisters. But on the days that Norma was not home, the resourceful little girls sneaked into her house and stole just enough food to soothe their hungry bellies and grab a little extra for their baby brothers.

Watching her mother and siblings scrounge for food and seeing her little brothers wearing old jeans and tattered shirts tormented Irma. If she had extra money, she shrewdly bought clothes for them. When buying clothes for Jody, Irma intentionally purchased some of the clothing too large or too small. The large ones were for James, only two years older than Jody, and the small ones were for Carl, Mildred, and Heber's last child born a year after Jody.

While Heber's children depended on others for food and clothing, he cared only for himself. About a year after selling the farm, Heber grew tired of his girlfriend and announced that he was moving to Miami to work for the Civilian Conservations Corps. He could tell Mildred anything, and she believed him. Mildred must not have read the newspapers or followed current events, or she would have known that the CCC operated from 1933 to 1942 in the United States and employed unmarried men ages seventeen to twenty-eight. Heber was forty-seven years old in 1948 and could not have been working with the CCC in Miami. The CCC story was one big lie, and Mildred believed it. While Heber was in Miami, he and Mildred exchanged letters, each with a common theme: money. In response to a letter Mildred sent to Heber, Heber wrote this letter on November 11, 1948:

Dear Mildred & All,

Rec. your letter. Was glad to hear from you all and to no [sic] you are all well. I was surprised to hear you say that you had spent that $100.00 I left with you. I have been gone only a little over 2 months. I have sent you over a 100.00 and you have spent the 100.00 I left with you. That is 100.00 a month. How come it takes so much more when I am not there. It did not take that much to live when I was there. How many more rugs have you bought? You no [sic] I am only one person and sometimes I can't work for misery. I am only making $50.00 per week. Looks like I am going to have to have some help in some way if it takes $100.00 per month for you to live. Now my advice to you is let Frannie look after the kids and you get you a job so you can help take care of you. Get you a job so you can help me take care of the expenses. Other women work so why can't you help me. Don't sit there and perish to death if it takes $100.00 a month for you. I just can't furnish it. I would if I could. I will do all I can but I am going to expect you to help me, which I think is only fair. The Dr. wants me to go to the hospital for 2 weeks and said he could cure me but I am not able. Altho I would give thousands of dollars not to ever have another one of those pains. I will close.

With much love to you and the kids.
As Ever, Heber

Heber's contrived sentiment, "With much love to you and the kids," meant nothing to Mildred, who required much more than Heber's insincerity; she needed cash. Confused by Heber's refusal to send her one hundred dollars a month when he admitted to making fifty dollars a week, Mildred wondered where Heber spent his extra money. It wasn't long before Mrs. L.C. Coleman answered Mildred's question when she wrote Mildred a letter:

Dear Friend,
December 15, 1948

I know you don't know me personally but you probably have heard about me. I'm Lawrence Coleman's wife, Ruth Grantham's sister-in-law. I'm writing in regard to Heber, your husband, and what he did down here and how many girls he went with. It wasn't any of my business until he started coming here and keeping my husband Ace out all night long. He has done this 4 times since he has been down here when Ace would have been at home. He has never stayed out all night before.

I asked Heber today twice to stay away from Ace as he always came 15 miles to get with Ace. Ace has his first time yet to go to South Miami after Heber as I told Heber and he knows it is the truth.

He and Ace were out all night long with two women Saturday night two weeks ago. That is what Heber's landlord said he told her, and twice there were calls to our phone from women wanting to know Heber's address. I told Heber I was going to write to you if he didn't stay away, if he came back.

I didn't bother in his or your affairs until Heber came messing with mine. So now I've got a bait of it and I'll stop him if I have to call the law for him interfering with peace in my family.

He is out here now down at the bar, comes 15 miles to get with Ace. So I'm sick and tired of him coming after Ace and staying out with women two or three times a week. He tried to go with an 18-year-old girl down here. He told her he wasn't married and when Simmie Madray told her Heber was married, Heber got mad at her for telling the girl he was married.

So you can do what you want to take what you please from him. It's none of my business but when he comes between me and Ace, then I'm going to give him hell as I am sick of him coming here after Ace.

Ace said he would not go if it was not for Heber coming here every other Saturday night. Heber is going to stop it or Ace is going to regret the day he ever started running around with your husband. If you just knew all the things I know on him that people have told me and what I have seen with my own eyes.

Will close now,
Mrs. L.C. Coleman
Miami, Florida

After Mrs. L.C. Coleman exposed Heber's lie and adulterous lifestyle, Mildred finally took matters into her own hands. Mildred explained to her great-granddaughter, Lori, how she acquired the money to rent a house with electricity:

"I knew that Heber had loaned some money to a man, so while he was gone working with the C.C.C. (Civilian Conservation Corps), I went to that man and asked him to pay the money back to me instead of to Heber. He did. And I used the money to rent a house in Jesup with electricity but no indoor toilet. Heber was good-for-nothing. He was just as happy when he had no job as when he did."

After returning from Miami and "working with the CCC," Heber soon learned why "it takes so much more when I am not there" when he discovered Mildred and the children had moved out of the shack and were living in a rental house. Not only had Mildred made a move without telling him, but she also committed him to monthly payments he could not afford, and he was livid. Unable to keep a job long enough to pay the rent, Heber received permission to relocate his family into his friend's goat barn, an act driven by selfishness, anger, and revenge to teach Mildred never to defy him again.

Mildred recalled her life with Heber during her interview with Lori but did not tell her of the suffering she and the children endured in the "goat house." The horrors there may have been too painful for Mildred to relive. Or Mildred could have chosen to spare her great-granddaughter from the gruesome details.

Mildred did not tell Lori that the goat house was nothing but a crude, unpainted barn made of wood slats spaced far enough apart to see through. She did not tell Lori that there were no walls or doors in the goat house, and the children slept in beds pushed closely together, and they heard sounds coming from Heber and Mildred no child should ever hear as they clung to each other in fear.

She did not tell Lori that in the goat house, Heber doubled over in pain, yelling "Goddamnit!" over and over again when the neurological side effects of untreated syphilis raged throughout his body and his outbursts terrified his children. And Mildred did not tell Lori about the unforgettable day she witnessed Heber beat her son and decided to do something about it.

Mildred had no telephone to call for help, so she walked into town and called Irma to report what Heber had done. Hearing her mother say Heber severely beat her five-year-old little brother James, Irma grew weak and wanted to throw up. The memories of her beatings flooded her mind.

Mildred disclosed to Irma that in a drunken rage the night before and without provocation, Heber whipped James so severely that his back looked like beef steak and pleaded with her to come quickly. Irma calmed her tormented mother and assured her that she and Frankie were on the way.

When Irma and Frankie entered the goat house, its stench and the smell of alcohol still on Heber's breath permeated the air. Irma's heart pounded when she confronted Heber, still fearful of his strap. But she was a grown woman now, and if she had to, she would defend herself and her helpless little brother. Poor James, the one Heber nicknamed "Buddy," was still whimpering in pain from the lashing.

Frankie and Irma found strength in one another and admonished Heber for what he had done to their brother. Heber had given Frankie suitcases to carry to nursing school and was furious with her when he shouted, "I want my goddamn luggage back!" as alcohol-infused sputum sprayed from his beet-red face. Frankie held firm, telling him she had enough money saved to buy new suitcases and she didn't need his old luggage.

Heber realized he was outmatched by his brave daughters and did not try to stop them as they carried Buddy to the car. After a stop by the hospital, where Irma and Frankie cleaned and dressed the wounds on Buddy's back, the sisters relocated their little brother to Doctortown until Heber was gone.

In 1949, there were no laws to protect children from abusive parents. Lawyers and local law enforcement agencies were the only recourse available for battered children. Irma remembered the kindness shown to her by Uncle Claude in 1941, the night Heber beat her when she was fourteen. Irma recalled that he called a lawyer, Mr. Doug Thomas, and she needed his help again.

The sight of the little boy's mutilated back must have infuriated Mr. Thomas, who had seen strap marks on Irma's body only a few years earlier. Before Mr. Thomas filed a formal complaint against Heber, he drove out to the goat house to present Heber and Mildred with an ultimatum: Heber must move out, and Mildred must find a suitable home for herself and her children, or he would begin legal proceedings to remove the children.

There was no way Mildred would choose Heber over her children; he had to go. With his reclaimed suitcases, Heber fled back to Miami, and Mildred and her four children relocated into governmental subsidized housing, "the projects," with Irma and Frankie's help.

The BB Quartet: Vallie May is seated in the middle. Standing behind her, *left to right:* Melissy, Puddin, Edna, and Annette. Circa 1949.

CHAPTER 6

A Welcomed Breeze

AFTER IRMA'S MOTHER AND SIBLINGS settled into the projects and Heber was back in Miami, life seemed to get a little better for Puddin and Melissy. Their memories of attending The Church of God with Norma on Sundays, squirming during the "fire and brimstone" sermons, and rocking out when the congregation sang peppy southern gospel hymns are still vivid in Melissy's mind.

Melissy says she "lives in gratitude" because of the wisdom attained from one of the hymnals she sang in church: "Give Me the Roses While I Live," written by R.H. Cornelius and James Rowe, copyright 1925.

Wonderful things of folks are said
When they have passed away
Roses adorn their narrow bed
Over the sleeping clay

Give me the roses while I live
Trying to cheer me on
Useless are flowers that you give
After the soul has gone

Let us not wait to do good deeds
Till they have passed away

Now is the time to sow good seeds
While here on earth we stay

Give me the roses while I live
Trying to cheer me on
Useless are flowers that you give
After the soul has gone

Kind words are useless when folks lie
Cold in a narrow bed
Don't wait till death to speak kind words
Now should the words be said

After the girls attended a few Sunday services with Norma, Vallie May Watkins, a kind, caring piano player, became enamored with the Robinson girls and their appreciation of music. When she asked them to join a singing quartet, the girls gladly accepted her invitation along with two other sisters, Edna and Annette, who also attended the Church of God. Little did they know that as they traveled throughout South Georgia to gospel shows for a twenty-five-dollar performance fee, Vallie May and the quartet would transport Puddin and Melissy to a world they had never seen before, a world where people lived in grand homes, wore clean new clothes, had plenty of food, and drove new cars.

Accompanied by Vallie May on the piano, with Puddin, Edna, and Annette singing backup, little Melissy often stole the show with her rap-like performance of stories from the Bible. Wearing matching black skirts, crisp white blouses, and black neckties Edna and Annette's mother made for them, the BB Quartet (booster band) often "boosted" for Hovie Lister and the Statesmen Quartet, a well-known Southern gospel group in the 1950s.

During one of the BB Quartet engagements, Hovie caught a glimpse of Melissy's starstruck eyes staring at his shiny Cadillac and offered to take the girls for a ride. More than seventy years later, Melissy remembers cruising with Vallie May and the BB Quartet around town in Hovie's Caddy, feeling like a princess in her stage outfit. And she remembers the day she announced she was old enough to drive and decided to have a little fun.

It was 1954; Frankie had graduated from nursing school in Savannah and accepted a nursing position at the hospital in Jesup. When thirteen-year-old Melissy discovered that Frankie parked her car at the hospital while she worked, she convinced Puddin to "borrow" it for a joyride with their friends. Puddin liked the idea until she asked her sister who would chauffeur them around. When Melissy answered, "I will!" reluctantly, Puddin went along for the ride.

When the agreed-upon day arrived, the mischievous girls slinked into the hospital parking lot and stealthily climbed into Frankie's automobile. With the spare key they confiscated days before, Melissy cranked Frankie's car, and she and Puddin absconded in it without detection. After gathering a few of their girlfriends, the girls bounced down the streets of Jesup, having the time of their lives with Melissy at the wheel.

Puddin and Melissy would have gotten away with the caper if Frankie's friend had not seen her car recklessly rolling down Cherry Street in Jesup and asked Frankie if she had been drinking and driving. Peeved at the woman's ridiculous question, Frankie challenged her friend and explained that she couldn't have seen her on the day in question because her car remained at the hospital all day while she worked. Further debunking the ridiculous accusation, Frankie approached the woman nose to nose, pointed her finger at her, and shouted, "I do not drink alcohol!"

Bewildered by the woman's bizarre observation and her insistence that Frankie must have been drunk the day her automobile rambled through town, Frankie wondered: *Who in the hell was driving my car?* It wasn't long before Frankie had the answer: The same sneaky little bandits that slipped undetected into Norma's house and ransacked her refrigerator were the same ones weaving through town in Frankie's car.

When Frankie shared with Irma that Puddin and Melissy had taken her car, "Mama Irma" had a long talk with the girls and admonished them for their dangerous prank. Fearing the girls might get into more serious trouble if she wasn't around to keep an eye on them, Irma decided it was time for her and Joe to leave Doctortown and move to Jesup.

In 1954 when Irma began house-hunting, the United States was experiencing a postwar housing boom in the suburbs, and housing was readily available for families eager to live the American dream. Irma's timing could not have been any better, and it didn't take long for her to find the perfect two-bedroom, one-bath bungalow in Shamrock, one of Jesup's new subdivisions. But persuading Joe to buy the house proved much more challenging than finding it. Joe, always the "bean counter," declared they didn't have enough "beans" to purchase the house in town. Irma's argument that they could borrow beans for the down payment and grow more beans for the monthly payments won Joe over.

Thanks to Irma's diligence, Joe, Irma, Jody, and Sandra said goodbye to Doctortown. The family, destined for good luck, moved into a gray house with red kitchen countertops and new appliances on the corner of Clover and Shamrock Street. My siblings and I have joked over the years that without our mother's drive, determination, and the good luck she found in Shamrock on Clover Street, we would have lived in the Doctortown house our entire childhood while our dad counted beans and our mother cooked on the old wood-burning stove.

Irma and Joe loved their new life in the city and their trips to the Jesup Drive-In with Jody and Sandra. Snuggled in the back seat with pillows, blankets, and popcorn, Jody and Sandra rarely kept their eyes open until the movie was over. But it didn't matter that they missed the ending; the fun was watching "TV" in their car. The Jesup Drive-In opened in 1948 and still operates today. It is one of three hundred remaining drive-ins in the United States, compared to about four thousand in the late '50s.

Another of Joe's and Irma's memorable activities also involved the family automobile. Because Jekyll Island, Georgia, opened to the public in 1948 and was only about an hour's drive from their home in Jesup, Joe, Irma, and their children made day trips in the summer there. Swimming in the ocean, playing in the sand, grilling burgers on the beach, and returning home in the dark with their suntanned kids fast asleep in the back seat were treasured memories for Joe and Irma.

During those early years in Jesup, there were lots of good times but there were a few bad times, too, one of which involved Sandra, Frankie, and a fire. One day while Frankie was recuperating at Joe and Irma's with a broken leg, five-year-old Sandra had the most innocent thought: *I wonder what would happen if I set something on fire?* While Frankie wasn't looking, Sandra grabbed a book of matches and skipped over to the neighbor's house to find out. Within minutes, Mr. Cunningham's garden was ablaze, and Sandra couldn't run home to Aunt Frankie fast enough.

Sandra doesn't remember much after the garden went up in flames other than Aunt Frankie's leg was broken and wasn't any help with the fire, eventually extinguished by Mr. Cunningham. And she doesn't recall much about another fire other than she did not intentionally start it.

While the family was away from home in early 1958, a small, smoldering fire ignited in the center of the house on Clover Street. I don't remember anything about the fire because my mother was pregnant with me. But Sandra does and says she has no idea why she put a rug over the furnace positioned deep in the floor before the family left home.

But I think I know why. The hideous grate covering the three-by-six hole in the hall floor was unsightly, and nine-year-old Sandra wanted to cover it up, unaware that the rug would catch on fire and take the life of their family's Boston terrier, Rocky. They found him under a bed, where he appeared to have fallen asleep after succumbing to smoke inhalation.

Because of Sandra's everlasting love for Rocky, she has always filled her homes with dogs. The first three were Boston terriers named Archie, Rocky, and Oreo. Sandra reminds me that D-O-G spelled backward is G-O-D and that dogs come into our lives when we need them the most. I guess she needed a little rock and roll when Elvis, the "singing" chihuahua, joined her family.

Sandra never forgot Rocky, the impetus for her deep affection for dogs. Although Rocky did not survive, the little bungalow and the old furnace on Clover Street did. Fortunately, the damage was all smoke-related, and my pregnant mother scrubbed all the soot off the walls just in time to give birth to me.

After the fire, life returned to normal for Joe and Irma. And finally, there was good news from Mildred. She had a job at the new elementary school in Jesup, and for a brief time, she did not depend on Heber for money. But it wasn't long before Mildred's worsening mental state forced her to rely on Heber again. Mildred shared her memories of her first and only job during her interview with Lori when she said:

"I would tell him that he ought to go out and look for work, that work would not come to him. I told him I would work if I could, but I couldn't with four school-age children at home. I did work for a while in the lunchroom at the new T.G. Ritch Elementary School. But I was often too sick to work."

When Mildred said she was often too sick to work, she referred to the days when depression overwhelmed her, leaving her inactive and unable to function. Desperate for help, Mildred confided in Mrs. Baker, the lunchroom manager, and disclosed that Heber refused to give her money to pay the household expenses and that she rarely had enough food to feed her children.

Mrs. Baker must have pitied her employee and cared enough to help her. When she disclosed Mildred's predicament to her husband, he scheduled a meeting with Herbert Strickland, an attorney. Confident that Heber could not throw her out of her rent-free subsidized house, Mildred agreed to meet with Mr. Strickland.

Before the meeting, Mildred contacted Heber's father, Monroe Robinson, and asked him to accompany her to Mr. Strickland's office. Monroe disapproved of his sorry, no-good son's despicable behavior, and he gladly went with Mildred to speak to the lawyer. With Monroe's blessing, Mr. Strickland filed charges against Heber for failure to support his family and deserting them.

Judge Thomas heard the case of Mildred Robinson vs. Heber Robinson and ordered Heber to pay forty-five dollars a month for child support. Thumbing his nose to the judge, Heber declared that it would be a "cold day in Hell" before Mildred got any more of his money. That cold day in Hell never came, but many cold days behind bars did when Judge Thomas sentenced Heber to twelve months in Reidsville State Prison for desertion in 1954.

After Heber went to prison, Mildred's mental health dramatically declined. Puddin and Melissy disclosed to Irma that they were free to do anything they wanted and that their mother was not taking care of them. They divulged to Irma that Mildred was in a dreadful state, and they did not know what was wrong with her.

They explained to their big sister Irma that their ungroomed mother spent days lying in a dark room with the curtains drawn, grimacing at the tiniest sliver of light that slipped through, and during the dark days when Mildred was in what they called a "mood," she did not speak, eat, or bathe. The girls revealed that their mother often suddenly awakened in the middle of the night, full of energy, unaware that she had been unresponsive for days, and began placing pots and pans on the stove as if she was cooking.

Puddin and Melissy told Irma that their mother had no food to cook when she awakened and they were eating at Norma's. They admitted they were angry with their mother because she did not care for them as the other mothers cared for their friends. And they confessed to Irma that they resented their mother's apathy and inability to make decisions for herself and that they were ashamed of her.

Irma recognized that Puddin and Melissy and their two young brothers were not safe living with Mildred during her bouts of depression so she came up with a solution to the problem: Her brothers and sisters would move in with Joe and her, keeping them safe each time Mildred slipped into a "mood." The four children shuffled back and forth from their two homes, living with Mildred during her highs and with Irma and Joe, their surrogate parents, during Mildred's lows. While caring for the children, Irma and Joe regularly delivered meals to Mildred to ensure she was eating.

During the time Puddin lived with Irma and Joe, she worked as a waitress at a restaurant in Jesup. And as she had done for Frankie, Irma found the job for her teenage sister. Because fourteen-year-old Melissy was not old enough to have a paying job, she worked as Irma and Joe's housekeeper and Jody's babysitter. The arrangement worked very well until the day Irma came home from work and found Jody crying and locked out of the house. When Irma questioned Melissy about why she did not let Jody come inside, Melissy honestly replied, "I am tired of him making a mess after I cleaned the house, so I just locked him out." Little Jody never went outside again while his mother was away and Aunt Melissy was babysitting.

Puddin and Melissy knew they had responsibilities in the Hodge household and they rarely disobeyed their big sister Irma. They were thankful for Irma and her comfortable home. Living with Irma and Joe was nothing like the impoverished life they left behind in the projects. When dining with Irma at Morrison's Cafeteria during a trip to Savannah, the girls felt as if they were in a five-star hotel.

Puddin worked two more jobs in clothing stores before graduating from high school, marrying, and moving away, leaving Melissy behind with Irma, but not for long. Melissy soon joined Puddin when she was fifteen years old to babysit Puddin's newborn baby.

"We all helped each other, and I think that is semi-typical. The oldest always helped the next one. Nobody talked about it. It was a given that we were to do that," Puddin told me.

Young Puddin and Melissy did not comprehend that with Irma's help, they were pulling themselves out of dire circumstances that could have easily defined the rest of their lives. Living with Irma and Joe transformed the sisters from a life of despair to one of hope. And at the Strand Theater in Jesup, they vicariously lived a glamorous one.

With a nickel in their hands and big grins on their faces, one Saturday the girls purchased a ticket at the Strand to watch movie stars Marge and Gower Champion. While viewing *Everything I Have Is Yours*, starring Marge and Gower, Melissy believed the film's announcer when he proclaimed, "You'll live with them. You'll dance with them. You'll even feel like a champion!" After the movie, inspired by Marge and Gower's enchanting on-screen lives, Melissy danced down Cherry Street, headed home to the projects, and vowed: *I'm going to be like that when I'm grown!*

"We saw the shining star on the hill. We just couldn't quite reach it when we were children," Puddin told me. One by one, Irma pushed her sisters—Frankie, Puddin, and Melissy—up the hill, rescuing them from a life of hardship, cruelty, and neglect, and served as the role model the girls desperately needed.

When I see my Aunt Frankie, the first question she always asks me is, "How are your mother and daddy?" They have always been and always will be in the forefront of her mind, even though my parents passed away years ago.

My mother must have been so proud of her little sisters who soared in her tailwinds. Irma had no "role model" to guide her through life, and she had no "idol" either. But Frankie, Puddin, and Melissy had both in their sister, Irma.

The fifteen-year-old girl aiding in the construction of World War II vessels carrying supplies overseas grew into a human vessel, transporting tender, fragile lives to a haven in her home and then out into the world.

I have always admired my mother for surviving the horrors she endured as a child to become a loving mother to her children and surrogate mother to her younger brothers and sisters. And it wasn't until she shared this story with me that I recognized she instinctively identified as "Mama" when she was a small child:

When Mildred contracted typhoid fever and became gravely ill, an ambulance rushed her to the hospital. While Mildred was away, five-year-old Irma decided she was "in charge" of her baby sister Frankie and said to her while pretending to prepare a meal, "Don't pull on Mama's dress; she's cooking supper."

From age five, the Vessel had been "in charge" of her siblings and had substituted as their "mama." After having children of her own, it was time for the Vessel to retire—but not before she made one more journey, this one to save her mother and two brothers.

With Irma's sisters thriving far away from their childhood homes, only two of Irma's siblings remained with their mother: the boys, ages twelve and eight. As Mildred's condition continued to deteriorate and her sons lacked any guidance or supervision, Irma arranged an evaluation for Mildred with a neurologist in Atlanta.

Irma hoped that a neurologist could diagnose her mother's mental condition and treat it so Mildred could take care of her only sons. But Irma and her sisters also needed to know why their mother wasn't assertive and outgoing, why she could not make any decisions for herself, why she could not stop Heber from abusing them, and why Heber so easily manipulated her all those years. And they needed to know if their mother's mood swings and diminished mental capacity were genetic. Mildred was about fifty years old when Irma carried her to the neurologist:

"I took Mama to Bessie Brannen to help her with these moods. Well, now it's termed manic depressive disorder. And I worked through Bessie at the health department and got the travel expenses paid to take her to Dr. Fincher in Atlanta, one of the best neurologists anywhere.

"I don't know who kept my children. Aunt Bell must have kept them. And I spent the night with Frankie, and I left Augusta and went to the doctor's office with Mama. I didn't know Atlanta back then any more than I knew New York.

"Without Mom in the room, Dr. Fincher asked me to begin as early as I could when I noticed these mood swings Mom had. I went back as far to the point as I could with this and how they affected her. And then he talked to her by herself. And I gave him all the history like I've told you of her birth and infancy, and so he must have talked with her for maybe forty-five minutes or an hour. We were there for a couple of hours, I guess.

"After I gave Dr. Fincher the history of Mom's birth and first few weeks of life, he said that when you're a baby, your brain is nourished just like your body. And obviously, that's her problem. Mom was not retarded in any way. Her brain never developed. Her manic-depressive disorder and diminished mental capacity were not something she was born with but developed. Dr. Fincher mailed me his diagnosis/report, and I took a copy of it to Bessie at the health department. It was a wonderful relief to all of us knowing that she didn't inherit her mental problems. My mom's birth mother was a very smart woman with a business head. Aunt Bell said that woman would do anything she wanted to do."

Irma and her sisters were relieved to learn that with medication to treat her bipolar disorder, their mother could function and take care of her sons. While Dr. Fincher's diagnosis confirmed for Mildred's children that their mother's mental illness was not genetic, it dealt a devastating blow to Mildred: Her brain was normal until her birth mother, Lula, one of "The Children in the Sawpit," did something unspeakable to it.

PART II
Lula Fights Back

Orphaned brother and sister, Harry and Lula.

CHAPTER 7

The Children in the Sawpit

A FAMILY LIVING NEAR ODUM in Brentwood, Georgia, found two children playing in a sawpit; the mother "took in" the girl, and her daughter and son-in-law "took in" the boy. When I heard those words, an image of unwanted children discarded like a litter of puppies was forever imprinted in my soul, and I had to learn more about them. It saddened me that my ancestors—my great-grandmother Lula, born in 1886, and my great-uncle Harry, born in 1884—were those two lost children.

I wasn't sure what a sawpit was, but I became convinced that it was not safe for children to play in one after researching Wikipedia. I learned that a sawpit was a hole dug into the ground used for positioning and sawing tree trunks into saw planks. The typical sawpit measured six feet wide, six feet deep, and fifteen feet long, large enough to house a full-grown man standing in it and maneuvering a long, two-handled "whip-saw" from below while another man manipulated the saw from above.

I had many questions: How old were Lula and Harry when found in the sawpit? Did Lula and Harry playfully enter the pit themselves, or were they purposely thrown into it with no way to escape? And if someone did callously force them into the sawpit, who could have committed such a cruel act? Or was the sawpit story nothing more than a silly anecdote passed down by the Moody family who found them? If the Moodys did discover my ancestors in the sawpit, I needed to believe that their birth parents deserted their children because they could not provide for them, and knew that Lula and Harry would be better-off with the Moody family. Indigence, sickness, or even death may have left Lula and Harry's biological mother and father no other choice but to abandon their children in the sawpit for the well-off Moodys to find. In the 1800s and early 1900s, it was common for wealthy families to take in orphaned children or children whose parents could not take care of them.

Looking for answers to my questions concerning Lula and Harry would require much investigation and, for fun, a little imagination. I first imagined that Lula and Harry were riders on an orphan train that may have passed through Wayne County, Georgia, and home of the sawpit where the Moodys allegedly found them.

The orphan trains transported orphaned and homeless children from crowded eastern cities of the United States, predominantly New York and Boston, to foster homes in rural areas. The trains operated between 1854 and 1929 and relocated about 250,000 children. The orphan train program placed more than three hundred children in Georgia.

When Lula and Harry were born in the mid- to late 1800s, typhoid fever, yellow fever, and flu epidemics left hundreds of children without parents and forced them to live on the streets. Some children, sadly, were abandoned by their parents because of severe poverty or alcohol abuse. In 1854, up to 34,000 children, referred to as "street rats" by the police, aimlessly roamed northeastern America's city streets, stealing and begging for food. Overcrowded orphanages failed to give these street rats a home.

Social activism and awareness of New York City's orphans' hopeless lives inspired Minister Charles Loring Brace to action. Brace, a graduate of Union Theological Seminary and Yale University, convinced that institutional care was not the solution to the orphanage crisis and believing that children would do well only in a family setting, devised a plan.

In 1853, at the age of twenty-seven, Brace founded the orphan train movement that operated for more than seventy-five years. Brace believed that by transporting children to American pioneers, they could live with families on farms, ridding the city streets of them.

The first orphan train departed Boston in 1850 with thirty children heading to Vermont and New Hampshire. In 1854, another train pulled out from New York City with forty-five children en route to Dowagiac, Michigan. Before children boarded the orphan trains, chaperons bathed the orphans, dressed them in new clothes, and pinned a name tag on their coats.

The orphan train cars provided no comfort for the displaced children, who were forced to sit on wooden benches and sleep on the floor. The juvenile riders were cramped into unheated cars like cattle and fed only once a day between stops in towns and communities that received prior notice of the train's arrival. Some prospective families chose their children from a list of the orphans on the train, and others adopted their children instantaneously when the train stopped in their town.

Routinely, the orphan train chaperons took the children to a local theater to put them up on a stage for prospective parents to choose one of them. The phrase "up for adoption" is believed to have originated from this practice. Some of the children found loving homes, but some did not. Some of the farm families viewed the children as free labor and treated them as servants rather than as their children.

Did Lula and Harry courageously jump off an orphan train in Georgia, rejecting the humiliation of being "put up" on a depot platform or a theater stage in city after city for prospective parents to poke and prod? I needed to obtain a United States Census that recorded Lula and Harry's birthplace to prove or disprove the orphan train theory. But finding one would not be easy.

When my mother shared stories about her grandmother Lula, Mildred's birth mother, she referred to her grandmother as Lula Daniel, believing that the Daniel family adopted her uncle Harry Daniel and her grandmother Lula. My earliest searches for Lula Daniel turned up nothing. However, I found a marriage certificate for Lula Moody. Still, my mother insisted that Lula's maiden name was Daniel, not Moody, so I redirected my search from Lula to Harry, hoping to find them living together in the Daniel home.

My hunt for Harry Daniel immediately bore the sweetest fruit. The Twelfth United States Census for Wayne County, Georgia, enumerated on June 20, 1900, recorded Harry in the home of Filmore and Ida Daniel, with no mention of his sister, Lula, living in the same household.

The 1900 census was the first census I had ever seen. The simple format and handwritten entries reminded me of how long ago Lula and Harry lived and inspired me to dig deeper and search harder for Lula. But I did not know her adopted name, and I did not know where to begin looking for her. But to my delight, I found Lula right under my nose when taking a second look at the census. The same 1900 census that recorded Harry as the adopted son of Filmore and Ida Daniel recorded Lula as the adopted daughter of Miriam Moody. I remember running from my writing office shouting: "I found her! I found her!"

With extraordinary luck, I discovered that related but different families adopted Lula and Harry. That explains why Harry's surname is Daniel and Lula's maiden name is Moody. The 1900 census for Wayne County, Georgia, recorded "Lula Fulcher" as the fourteen-year-old adopted daughter of Miriam Moody and "Harry Fulcher" as the sixteen-year-old adopted son of Filmore and Ida Daniel. I had a birth name—"Fulcher!"

Inspired by my discovery, I searched for an 1890 census that would have recorded Lula and Harry at ages four and six and placed them in either their Fulcher birth home or their adoptive homes. But my hopes of finding them went up in smoke when I learned that the 1890 census burned in 1921. Since the United States did not issue birth certificates at the time of their births, I found no documents identifying Lula and Harry's biological parents.

The 1900 census is the only record I uncovered of Lula and Harry's existence before they married and moved out of their adoptive homes. And although it is a treasure trove of information, it also derailed my orphan train theory. The census states that Lula and Harry were born in Georgia, and since orphan trains originated in northeastern cities, Lula and Harry could not have been orphan train riders.

The tale of my ancestors jumping off an orphan train and landing in the sawpit proved to be nothing but a figment of my imagination. I would have to find another explanation for how Lula and Harry ended up in the sawpit.

So again, armed with only my thoughts interfaced with the 1900 census, I fantasized another theory of Lula and Harry's adoption, and it involved Filmore Daniel, Harry's adoptive father. Filmore was born in North Carolina, coincidentally the same state the 1900 census records as the birthplace of Lula and Harry's biological mother. Filmore possibly knew Lula and Harry's birth mother; she may have been one of his three sisters or perhaps a friend he knew when he lived in North Carolina.

Lula and Harry's biological parents may have died or been unable to care for their children, and Filmore agreed to take them. But if Filmore did not know Lula and Harry's birth mother and was not the connection between the children and the Moodys, was there another explanation for their adoption?

Maybe Lula and Harry were a Moody family member's illegitimate children born to a woman who could not care for them and whose last name was Fulcher. Rather than admit one of their own fathered children in an adulterous affair, the Moodys may have created the sawpit tale.

Or it is plausible that either one or both of the Fulchers knew David Moody, the man who found them. The Fulchers and David may have determined the best home for Harry was with David's sister Ida and her husband, Filmore Daniel. And the best home for Lula was with David's widowed mother, Miriam.

But there is another explanation for the confusion surrounding Lula and Harry, and it is the hardest one for me to accept: They were discarded like unwanted puppies in the sawpit. One or both of Lula and Harry's Fulcher parents may have walked away, disappearing forever, leaving their children in the sawpit until someone found them.

Harry's wife and son, Lela and Vernon Daniel holding hands for a professional photograph. Circa 1922.

CHAPTER 8

Good Fortune

HARRY'S ADOPTIVE FATHER, Filmore Daniel, migrated to Georgia from North Carolina when he was a young man, probably seeking work and a wife. When he crossed paths with Ida Moody, he acquired both.

Ida Moody was a third-generation descendant of the founding members of the Moody family in Wayne County, Georgia. Ida's great-grandfather Isaac A. Moody Sr., born in 1774 in South Carolina, traveled to Georgia and settled in Wayne County's wilderness.

In June 1979, the descendants of Isaac A. Moody compiled the history book entitled *The I.A. Moody Family*. The book's foreword describes the early beginnings of Ida's Moody family:

> When the wilderness country of Georgia was settled, the Pioneers were forced to live under very primitive conditions, which could not be imagined by those of us born in this century. These people learned lessons in living the hard way, through trial and error. Courage, resourcefulness, independence, along with hard work were all traits of these hardy people. Above all, a steadfast faith in God helped them to surmount the many obstacles and problems which faced

them daily. Poor in the wealth of material possessions and money, but rich in neighborliness, patience and kindness, the essentials of life were common traits.

Lifestyles were plain in home and dress, no frills or puffs. Very little, if any, structural schooling was afforded, and in the main, most would have been considered uneducated or illiterate. It is indeed an honor to have been a descendant of these brave God-fearing men and women. We can be proud of our heredity.

With the combination of hard work and gifts of timber and turpentine from the land of pines, generation after generation of Moodys prospered. By the late 1800s, crude cabins dotted the bucolic Georgia landscape, many built by the early Moody settlers. The homes were primitive and lacked few conveniences other than a fireplace for cooking meals and cots for sleeping.

Not long after arriving in Georgia, Filmore Daniel must have taken a hard look at the bare-bones dwellings built by the brave Moody pioneers and undoubtedly desired a larger, better place for himself and his new bride. Because Filmore's father was a carpenter, Filmore may have learned enough carpentry skills from him to erect a structure with divided rooms and a kitchen on the timberland given to Ida by her Moody family. Ida and Filmore's large home stood out among the modest ones in the Georgia pines and became known as "the big house."

Filmore would have been very proud of his creation, but ironically, the "big house" may have served as a constant reminder that he could not "fill more" children in it. Year after year passed without the joy of welcoming a new baby, and the childless couple may have lost all hope of ever having a child until Harry Fulcher appeared.

What a joyful day it must have been when Ida and Filmore first laid eyes on Harry. Showered with love, affection, and the security of a stable home, Harry grew into a very handsome, well-adjusted man. He towered over six feet tall with a head full of wavy brown hair and a lean, muscular body. His good looks attracted the local girls, but only one girl glowed exceptionally bright in Harry's eyes.

She was Lela Moody, Ida's cousin. Ida would have been delighted when her son announced that he and Lela were getting married. Because Harry was adopted, he and Lela were not genetic cousins. However, they probably would have married anyway with Ida's and Filmore's blessings since it was common for cousins to marry cousins in rural America, where meeting and courting spouses within the family circle was convenient.

Harry's wife, Lela, was the third of fifteen children and oldest daughter of I. A. Moody III, "Sonny," and Lucy Floyd, "Sis," Moody. Lela's Moody roots guaranteed Harry a secure position on the growing Moody family tree. Coincidentally, I. A. Moody III, Lela's father, is the same "Sonny" who married Mildred May's adoptive sister Nina years later.

Lela's father, Sonny, owned vast amounts of land, a turpentine and sawmill business, a cotton gin, and a large store that sold clothes, shoes, hardware, seeds, and farming tools. Sonny also served as the postmaster for the Brentwood Post Office for several years; his daughter, Lela, worked in the post office with him.

Friends of Sis and Sonny affectionately remember them as good parents who loved each other and their children very much. Harry was fortunate to marry into a family rich in worldly goods and love. And how wonderful it is that Harry's wife blessed him with his only child, Harry "Vernon" Daniel, in 1914.

There are photographs of Vernon when he was a child in the Moody family book with his mother, Lela. In one of the pictures, Vernon is about three years old and peeking over a large roll of fence wire on which his mother gracefully sits with her hands in her lap. She is wearing a wide-brimmed sun hat, a popular accessory in the early 1900s. The carefree mother and her little son appear relaxed and unbothered by the photographer's interruption of their playtime on the fence wire.

And the other photograph is a formal portrait of Vernon at about age eight, sporting a miniature dark suit, standing beside his mother, Lela. Lela is seated, wearing a pearl-enhanced scoop neck dress and a flower-adorned hat that lends an air of sophistication and wealth to her ensemble. Fine clothes for her family would have been easily accessible to Lela in her father's general store.

At the moment the camera captured their images, Lela and Vernon stared directly into the camera while clasping each other's hands, clearly bonded to one another. Harry must have been grateful that his only son's mother was a wonderful, caring woman who would never leave him, who would hold his hand. And unlike Harry, Vernon would never experience the pain of being separated from his mother.

Vernon blessed Harry and Lela with seven grandchildren, six boys and one girl. Vernon and his wife, Aline, named one of their twin boys Harry in honor of Vernon's father.

Given up so long ago and separated from his only sibling, Harry lived a much different life than his sister, Lula. Securely perched on the Moody family tree, Harry blossomed, anchored by its strong roots.

In *The I.A. Moody Family* book, there is proof of Harry's legitimacy as a Moody heir and the only child of Ida Penelope Moody and Filmore Daniel:

> Ida Penelope Moody, b. 1867, d. 1947, married Filmore Daniel, d. Abt. 1924.
> *Child: one son (adopted)*
> **Harry A. Daniel**, b. 5/8/1884, d. 5/11/1945, m. Lela Moody, daughter of Isaac A.
> and Lucy Floyd Moody.

In stark contrast to the documentation of Harry's legitimacy, the Moody family history book does not mention Lula. The 1900 census is the only evidence that Miriam adopted Lula. The Moody family history book should have recorded Lula as the adopted daughter of Miriam Moody along with Miriam's biological children, Ida, and David Moody. But it does not:

> Isham (Bud) Moody, b. 1834, d. 1889,
> married Miriam Samantha Tillman, b. 1838, d. 1930.
> *Children: Ida Penelope Moody, David Wadley Moody*

Lula's omission as Miriam's third child from the Moody history book could have been because, unlike Harry, Lula did not marry into the Moody family and lost contact with her adoptive mother, Miriam. Or another explanation for the absence of any record of Lula in the Moody book could be that Miriam never acknowledged Lula as her daughter and disowned her when she began dating men and spending nights away from home. Or Lula may have been nothing more to Miriam than a servant, rejected when she no longer needed her.

Miriam may have agreed to take Lula only because of the insistence of her children, Ida and David, after their father passed away. Ida and David may have encouraged their aging, widowed mother, Miriam, to adopt Lula and another child, John Floyd, to take care of her. John would have been responsible for the outside chores of gardening, chopping wood, and feeding the chickens and livestock, while Lula would have attended to Miriam and the inside duties. Lula's "family," in stark contrast to Harry's, consisted of an unrelated male and an aging widow. Becoming Miriam's domestic servant would not have been the best situation for Lula.

Observing Harry's parents treat him like a son and not as free labor could have been a source of heartache and jealousy for Lula. She may have longed to be a part of Harry's family. She may have wondered why Ida and Filmore did not choose her to be their little girl and why Miriam never treated her like a daughter. Filmore and Ida's decision not to adopt Lula along with Harry could have triggered the same feelings Lula may have had of not being good enough for her birth parents.

I wonder if Harry realized that his adoption blessed him with the good fortune of being accepted by two loving parents. And as he watched his sister become Miriam's handmaiden, I wonder if he experienced any guilt for having a mother and a father who showered him with unconditional love and expected nothing in return. Harry was Lula's older brother, and like most older brothers, he probably felt responsible for his little sister.

But Harry would have found solace in knowing that he could see his sister regularly; she and Miriam, Harry's adoptive grandmother, lived across the road from Harry's home with Filmore and Ida. Harry and Lula would have spent time together going back and forth to school. If they remembered their birth parents and missed them, Harry and Lula would have clung to one another and reassured each other while adjusting to their new homes.

But when Harry began courting Lela, Lula saw less and less of him and more of the adoring suitors drawn to her. Lula had become a lovely young woman with silky auburn hair, honey-brown eyes, and ivory skin. She reveled in her admirers' attention, but her playful interactions with them abruptly changed when she met Ronnie. Ronnie's slender body, tall frame, jet-black hair, and blue eyes excited a passion in Lula she had never experienced.

Lula should have listened to Miriam and her friend Nina Poppell, who advised her to find a good man who could provide for her. She should have paid more attention to the churning in her gut, reminding her that she had no home before Miriam adopted her. Driven by lust for Ronnie, Lula ignored Miriam's and Nina's advice and the sick feeling in her stomach when she began spending the night with Ronnie.

Miriam disapproved of Lula's behavior and demanded that she stop seeing Ronnie or move out of her house. Suddenly Lula found herself in a predicament that would affect the rest of her life: give up Ronnie and remain in her home with Miriam or continue seeing him without any promise of marriage and risk becoming homeless again. Her choice became much easier to make when Walter approached Lula with a proposal, and his timing could not have been any better.

Dr. Walter Marshall Odum's portrait that once hung in the halls of the hospital in Jesup, Georgia.

CHAPTER 9

A Windfall

WALTER MARSHALL ODUM had been infatuated with Lula for years without Lula ever showing any interest in him. Walter was handsome enough and intelligent enough, but he was not much taller than Lula, and he was a little chubby. Lula never considered him anything other than a friend, and he had no chance of ever stealing her away from Ronnie.

Walter and Lula attended school together in Odum, the community named after Walter's father, Godfrey Odum. Godfrey's obituary remembers him as "one of the wealthiest men in Wayne County." However, Godfrey's early start in life did not position him on a straightforward path to affluence and prosperity.

Born as one of ten children to James and Mary Odum in Bulloch County, Georgia, Godfrey lost his father when he was a boy, and before his sixteenth birthday, his mother died while on a trip to Savannah with her new husband. With his mother's death, Godfrey became orphaned and under the care of his court-appointed guardian, James Rimes.

Mr. Rimes arranged for Godfrey to depart his family home in Bulloch County, Georgia, to live with Ezekiel and Sarah Clifton in neighboring Emanuel County. Sharing the farm work with the Cliftons, Godfrey brought a pair of much-needed work hands. After years of living and working with the Cliftons, Godfrey set out on his long life's journey when he married Rebecca Ann Moody in 1856.

Soon after their marriage, Godfrey, Rebecca, and their firstborn, Vicey, relocated to Appling County, Georgia, later designated as Wayne County, Georgia. The 1860 census records Godfrey and Rebecca, both in their twenties, living in Appling County, Georgia, with five-year-old Vicey and a five-month-old child who later died in infancy.

When Godfrey settled his family in Wayne County, he raised and sold livestock, harvested timber from the land he owned, and procured more property with the proceeds earned from selling his trees. At times Godfrey purchased land, kept it a few years, sold it for a hefty profit, and then repurchased it.

By 1879, when he was forty-seven years old, Godfrey amassed enough money to buy 2,940 acres in the vicinity of the present town of Odum from Mr. Jim Poppell, Columbus Poppell's father and Mildred May's adoptive grandfather. Godfrey Odum probably shared a few cider drinks with his friend Jim as they discussed the land transfer.

Jim and Godfrey may have toasted the deal with more than cider when Jim agreed to sell his land for $3,500. A shot or two of whiskey would have been a more appropriate celebratory drink since Jim Poppell netted the equivalent of about $100,000 in today's purchasing power, and Godfrey Odum now owned all the land that was eventually named "Odum" in his honor.

Hazel Dean Overstreet in the 1985 Odum Homecoming program wrote:

"Mr. Odum was an able business man. An old history book in the possession of one of Mr. Godfrey Odum's grandsons, Mr. Genell Odum, of Odum, states that Mr. Odum in the year 1900 could command, upon a moment's notice, $10,000.00 (no little sum in those days) and owned a vast tract of land, consisting of twelve thousand acres (12,000)." (Ten thousand dollars in 1900 is equal to approximately $350,000 today.)

With so much money at his disposal, Godfrey would have provided a life of privilege for Rebecca and Vicey. But with money comes power, and Godfrey appears to have wielded his over Rebecca when he began having children with other women, three with Rachel Johnson and four with Victoria Moody, Walter's mother. Rachel maintained her household separate from Godfrey; however, their oldest child lived intermittently with both of them.

Unlike Rachel, Victoria Moody did not have her own home and lived with Godfrey and Rebecca as their servant when she began having Godfrey's children. The 1880 census records a twenty-eight-year-old servant named "V. Moody" (Victoria) living in Godfrey and Rebecca's household.

Since Victoria Moody and Rebecca Moody were born in the same county, they may have been related. An aging Rebecca and Godfrey in their forties may have summoned Rebecca's much younger relative to join them and become their housekeeper. Or possibly Victoria, having not married, needed a home. It is doubtful that Victoria knew that her duties as a servant would include serving as Godfrey's mistress.

A few years after moving in with Godfrey and Rebecca, Victoria gave birth to a son. During the following six years, Victoria, disguised as a domestic, delivered three more of Godfrey's sons.

I find it difficult to believe that Rebecca or Victoria was content with their living arrangement. While Rebecca shared her home and her husband with another woman for seventeen years, Victoria seems to have hidden in the shadows impersonating a housekeeper and a boarder while birthing Godfrey's children. Rebecca probably objected to Godfrey's relationship with Victoria but chose to accept it rather than face expulsion from her home. Godfrey's wealth would undoubtedly have been an incentive for both women to tolerate one another. Without education or income, women like Rebecca and Victoria depended on the men in their lives for survival.

Rebecca's cohabitation with Godfrey, Victoria, and her children and occasionally Rachel's children ended only with her death in 1897. Five years after Rebecca died, Godfrey married Victoria, probably at her insistence to secure her and their four sons' legitimacy and entitlement to Godfrey's estate. Godfrey was seventy years old, and Victoria was fifty when they married. Less than two years later, Godfrey was dead. Had they not married, Godfrey and Rebecca's only child could have inherited Godfrey's entire estate, leaving Victoria and her children and Rachel's children with nothing.

The fact that Godfrey fathered four sons with Victoria, and adopted his and Rachel's three children while still married to Rebecca must have been a closely guarded secret. There is no mention of Victoria and her children or Rachel Johnson's children in Godfrey's obituary. Or it is possible that Godfrey's only child with Rebecca, Vicey, may have contributed the information for the obituary and chose not to disclose her father's other wife and children. The following is an excerpt from Godfrey's obituary:

> Mr. Odum was married September 18, 1856, to Rebecca Ann, daughter of James and Eliza Moody, both natives of Liberty County, where they lived and died. Mr. and Mrs. Odum have had two children, one, Vicey, and another which died in infancy. In politics, Mr. Odum is a staunch democrat, and has served the county as justice of the inferior court for four years. He is a Master Mason. Mr. Odum is strictly a businessman, being prompt, and exacting promptness in all appointments and obligations. The post office and railway were named in his honor.

Godfrey Odum, age seventy-one, the wealthiest man in Wayne County, had no will; his heirs were not only left to divide his estate, but they would also have to prove their entitlement to it. On February 19, 1904, a week after Godfrey's death, James A. Morris was appointed administrator of Godfrey's estate. Over a year later, in June 1905, Victoria Moody Odum surfaced from the veils of a servant and boarder to make the following announcement and notice before the Ordinary of Wayne County:

I

That GODFREY ODUM, who at the time of his death and who for many years prior thereto was a citizen of said county, and state, departed this life at Milledgeville, Ga., where he had gone for treatment and care by physicians, on the fourteenth (14th) day of February 1904.

II

That said GODFREY ODUM, at the time of his death, was seized and possessed lands, money, notes and other personal property.

III

That said GODFREY ODUM and the undersigned L. VICTORIA ODUM had been legally joined in the holy bonds of matrimony several years ago and were husband and wife at the time of the death of said GODFREY ODUM.

IV

That said GODFREY ODUM died intestate leaving no will.

V

That said GODFREY ODUM left surviving him besides the undersigned widow, seven children, four by the undersigned widow, three by RACHEL JOHNSON, an unmarried female, said three children by RACHEL JOHNSON having been adopted by the said GODFREY ODUM during his lifetime and made capable of inheriting his estate, and one child by the first wife of said GODFREY ODUM, said first wife having departed this life many years ago. Said GODFREY ODUM besides the undersigned widow and seven children left no other descendants or representatives of children who died before him, the said widow and seven children being entitled to the estate of said deceased, GODFREY ODUM.

VI

And the said L. VICTORIA ODUM has elected and by this instruction and notification doth Elect to Claim, demand, have, receive and accept a "child's part" and that means to say a "one fifth" part and share in the estate of the said GODFREY ODUM, in lieu of and in place of dower and all rights thereof.

VII

Wherefore the said L. VICTORIA ODUM, upon the promises prays: that this her notification and her formal election and declaration to take said share of said estate instead of dower, she filed in said Court, be entered upon the docket thereof at this present term, that it be recorded on the minutes of the Ordinary and Court of Ordinary of said county to notify and in order to inform this court and the world and any legal representative appointed on said estate of her said election so to take such share in lieu of dower as herein set out, she having notified Jas. A. Morris of said state and County, duly qualified administrator of said estate of her election at the time of his qualification as administrator.

And may it please the Court to enter such judgment and make such order and perform and render all said ministerial acts and duties as shall be necessary and proper for the complete and perfect establishment and preservation of her rights by virtue of her said election made known to said administrator at the time of his qualification and now in said court so declared.

Respectfully, Victoria Odum

Victoria must have been a selfless woman, choosing to accept a child's part of the estate and establishing a claim for not only herself and her children but also for Vicey, Rebecca's child, and Godfrey's three adopted children. Because of her diligence and refusal to remain in the shadows any longer, Victoria won for herself and her children their fair share of Godfrey's wealth.

With the distribution of Godfrey's money and lands in 1905, Godfrey and Victoria's third son, eighteen-year-old Walter, became a very wealthy man. Awarded with a sizable amount of cash, farmlands, livestock, and a home in the neighboring community of Brentwood, Walter, still very much smitten with Lula, made her an offer she could not refuse. Walter promised Lula that if she waited for him and managed his farm until he finished medical school in Atlanta, they would live a well-to-do life in a grand house with servants when he returned home.

Taken with the prospect of an idyllic future that Ronnie could not give her, Lula broke off her relationship with him and chose money and security over love. In July 1905, nineteen-year-old Lula Moody married eighteen-year-old Walter Marshall Odum.

CHAPTER 10

A Hurricane Is Coming

WALTER'S TENDER HEART MUST have surged with love for the girl he admired for years and now was his. When he learned that Lula carried a deep secret into their marriage, his devotion to her did not waver. My mother recalled every detail of the story her Aunt Bell shared with her about Lula's relationship with Walter and then passed to me:

"When he married Grandma, obviously, she never let him touch her before they married. But on their wedding night, not only could he tell that she was not a virgin, he could tell she was pregnant. And he knew the child was not his. He loved Grandma so much. They say she was the prettiest woman in Wayne County and smart, and I believe it because even when she died, she was pretty. He said, 'Lou,' he called her Lou, 'that doesn't matter. I love you so much, and it will never be a problem. No one will ever know it but you and I.' In other words, the baby will come, and people would think it was his, and there would be no problem."

On January 6, 1906, Walter's birthday, Lula delivered a beautiful, healthy baby girl. And just as Walter promised, he professed to be the baby's father even though the child came six months after Lula and Walter married. The local gossip spread quickly that the baby they named Mildred May could not be Walter's and was Ronnie's.

Walter refused to allow anyone to undermine his undying love for Lula and supported and protected her from prying eyes and judgmental jabs of friends and relatives. Impervious to the nosey neighbors and their meddling, Walter's loyalty to Lula remained steadfast. Walter believed in Lula and trusted her to care for his farmland and home while away at medical school, and he had no reason to think that Lula would not be a loving mother to Mildred May and a faithful wife to him. And he could never have imagined what Lula would do after he returned to medical school.

Not long after the train pulled away from the station carrying Walter back to Atlanta, Lula approached Carrie, her handmaiden and servant, with a proposition: Disappear with Mildred May, never come back, and receive a hefty amount of cash. Believing that Carrie would obey her, Lula must have been stunned when she responded to Lula's offer with these chilling words: "Miss Lula, I can't take your baby. They'll lynch me if they catch me with money and a white child."

Unable to convince Carrie to leave with Mildred May, Lula became increasingly frustrated with the child she did not want and who prevented her from living a carefree lifestyle until, by chance, she discovered a solution to her problem. Lula observed that the laudanum drops, a form of the narcotic opium Walter instructed her to administer to Mildred May for colic and excessive crying, had a bonus effect. When Lula dropped the recommended amount onto Mildred May's tongue, the crying soon stopped, and Mildred May fell into a short, drug-induced sleep.

Each time Mildred May awakened, Lula administered more and more laudanum, lengthening the time Mildred May slept. While her child lay drugged and sleeping, Lula was free to stay out all night long. What happened next is best told in my mother's words:

"Dr. Odum had to go back to school, so he left Grandma to oversee the farm and the workers. And he had a big farm and horses in Brentwood, above Odum. Back in those days, they had people that worked for them. The baby came, and Grandma didn't settle down. Dr. Odum didn't come home too often, but Grandma was having a ball running around while he was gone. She was a beautiful woman, and she was as wild as she could be. She was like my daddy was."

Nina Poppell and Lula had been friends since they were in school together, but Nina vehemently disapproved of her friend's behavior. When Nina failed to convince Lula to stay home and care for her child, she felt helpless.

But help came from an unexpected source when Carrie, Lula's servant, reached out to Walter's mother, Victoria. Until Carrie visited Victoria, Nina had no idea that Lula was drugging and not regularly feeding Mildred May. Nina may have felt she was betraying her friend when she agreed to abduct Mildred May, but saving an innocent child's life would have been more important than her relationship with Lula.

While Nina risked losing Lula's friendship, Carrie risked losing her job and home to save the poor infant when she contacted Victoria. But Carrie knew she had to do something after weeks of discovering Mildred May unattended and unresponsive in the mornings, and she, too, put an innocent child's life above all else.

Carrie reported to Victoria that Lula fed Mildred May bottles spiked with laudanum so Lula could stay out all night. Carrie also shared with Victoria that she observed Lula placing more than one or two drops of laudanum in Mildred May's mouth. When my mother shared with me Carrie's report to Victoria, I noted that she referred to Mildred May as "the baby" and detached herself from the painful reality that "the baby" was her mother:

"And Carrie would come over there in the morning after Grandma had been out all night cattin' around. She would be lying there wet, legs messed up; Carrie would find the bottle sour and curdled. That bottle had been put in the baby's mouth so it wouldn't cry and she had been out all night. It was unbelievable. She'd leave that baby, stick a bottle in there and come back eight or nine hours later. When Dr. Odum came home after his mom sent for him, she laid it out from A to Z. That was how Aunt Bell put it. She told him what Lula had been doing for weeks."

Victoria did not appeal for and win Walter's share of Godfrey's estate to allow a two-timing tramp like Lula to benefit from it while she had affairs with other men and failed to properly care for his child. And above all, Victoria had been a good mother to her children; Lula's mistreatment of Mildred May would have been loathsome to Victoria. Learning of the massive amounts of laudanum Lula gave to Mildred May and hearing of Lula's overnight trysts while her baby lay sedated must have been more than Victoria could bear.

When Victoria "laid it out from A to Z" and told Walter about Lula's adulterous lifestyle, the nineteen-year-old man full of hopes and dreams died that day. Walter loved Lula unconditionally and trusted her with his home, his farm, his workers, and his heart. But she betrayed him, and he could not forgive the heartless woman he married.

When Victoria briefed Walter on the plan she and Caroline devised to excise Lula from her son's life and extricate Mildred May with one massive blow, he was all-in. Walter, Caroline, and Nina stood ready to do their part in removing Lula and freeing Mildred May.

To prevent Lula from suspecting that he was plotting against her, Walter would act as if he knew nothing of Lula's unfaithfulness and abuse of Mildred May. Walter needed to convince Lula that he missed her and the baby, and at the last minute, decided to take the next train home to spend a few days with them. Walter also must persuade Lula to leave Mildred May with Carrie while he and Lula had dinner with Victoria. Once Walter removed Lula from the house, Caroline and Nina could swoop in and grab Mildred May.

Victoria's plot worked flawlessly. As soon as Walter and Lula's buggy rolled down the road and out of sight, Caroline and Nina hastily entered Walter and Lula's home, snatched Mildred May, and vanished. Meanwhile, with Lula in tow, Walter stopped his buggy in the middle of Branchwood Creek. When my mother told me what happened next, I was hooked into the story and on the edge of my seat:

"So, the next day, sometime afterward, they were going to his mother's for a meal. You had to go through bodies of water. There were no bridges. I remember when we'd go to Aunt Bell's, that Branchwood Creek, we'd have to do that.

"And he stopped his horse and buggy in the middle of the creek en route. And he said: 'Lou, I forgot how your diamond looks.' And he took her hand and pulled it off, and when he got that, he started laying it out to her, the life she had been living while he was gone."

Lula was trapped, and Walter had her exactly where he wanted her, aware that if Lula tried to exit the carriage, she would step ankle-deep into the icy-cold creek water. Lula had no choice but to remain seated while Walter, fueled with anger and scorn, admonished her. Walter showed no sympathy for Lula and remained undeterred by her pleas for forgiveness and hollow promises to be a good and faithful wife and a better mother to Mildred May.

With Lula's ring in his pocket, Walter steered his buggy not to his mother's house for dinner as promised but to Miriam's house, where he ordered Lula out and forbade her to ever return to his property. As he turned the buggy around and headed home, Walter shouted these words: "You will never see Mildred May again!"

Walter M. Odum)
vs.   ) Libel for divorce.
Lula Odum   ) Wayne Superior Court, Nov term 1909.

The following jury was impaneled and sworn to try this case, viz:

1. H. J. Madray
2. Henry Hilton
3. D. S. Price
4. Isham Roberson
5. Geo Poppell
6. D. P. Taylor
7. D. R. Thornton
8. S. A. Strickland
9. H. J. Hilton
10. D. H. Roberson
11. Devin Westbury
12. R. B. Wilson.

And returned the following verdict to wit
We the jury find that sufficient proofs have been submitted to authorize the granting of a total divorce between the parties in favor of the defendant, that is to say a divorce a vinculo matrimonii upon legal principles. We further find in favor of the defendant the sum of three hundred and thirty three dollars and thirty three cents as permanent alimony. We further find in favor of the plaintiff the sum of Fifty Dollars as attorneys fees. We further find against the removal of the disabilities of the plaintiff. This 23d day of November 1909.

Walter Odum)
vs.   ) Libel for divorce, In Wayne
Lula Odum) Superior Court, November term 1909

It appearing to the Court, that the jury trying the above stated case, has returned a verdict in favor of the defendant for a total divorce, that is to say a divorce a vinculo matrimonii, upon legal principles: It is therefore, considered ordered and decreed by the Court that the defendant be and she is hereby decreed to be totally divorced from the plaintiff Walter M. Odum, and is hereby permitted to contract marriage again.

It is further ordered and decreed that the defendant Lula Odum, do have and recover of and from the plaintiff Walter M. Odum

CHAPTER 11

Gusts of Disgust

WALTER SEIZED EVERYTHING from Lula that day in the middle of Branchwood Creek—her marriage, her home, her affluent lifestyle, her ring, and her daughter—and he believed that he was free from her forever. But he was unaware that Lula possessed the strength to fight back. Undaunted by the shame and humiliation of getting caught cheating on her husband and nearly killing her child, Lula Moody Odum, the little girl found in the sawpit and the accused adulterous child abuser, did not accept defeat.

Nineteen-year-old Lula methodically crawled her way out of the hole she had dug for herself, starting with finding a place to live other than with Miriam. When she heard that a large family in the neighboring town of Glennville needed a woman to wash and iron their clothes, Lula found her ticket out of Odum. Refusing to live in shame, humiliation, and guilt, shunned by her friends and family, Lula accepted the position as George and America Anderson's laundress and took refuge in their home.

The thirty-mile, day-long journey by horse and buggy to the Anderson home provided plenty of time for Lula to reflect and process the events leading to her departure from Odum. Walter's voice shouting "You will never see Mildred May again!" must have played over and over in her head while traveling to Glennville, where she could start all over.

In Glennville, Lula would never see Walter's mother again or feel her disgust and hatred for her. In Glennville, Lula could hide from everything and everyone but her conscience. And in Glennville, Lula could become a new person, wiping away any memory of her past life.

Lula heard nothing from Walter for two years after leaving Odum. But that all changed when Walter filed for divorce in the Wayne Superior Court in February 1908. Walter's divorce petition ordered Lula to appear for the March 1908 term, but she was a no-show; the Wayne County sheriff could not locate and serve Lula since she did not reside in Wayne County.

Three months passed before Walter's attorney found Lula in Glennville and presented the petition to her attorney, who signed and acknowledged its legal service. Also, Lula and her attorney waived Wayne Superior Court's jurisdiction and agreed to a hearing of the case in its next term. Three days later, Lula filed an answer to Walter's divorce petition, denying all his allegations against her and stating that his charged adultery acts against her were untrue.

While waiting for the next term of the Wayne Superior Court, Lula filed a petition for temporary alimony and counsel fees on August 22, 1908; she also asked for an injunction against Walter's disposing of any of his property. In response to Lula's plea, Walter argued that because Lula was a resident of Tattnall County and not Wayne County, his divorce suit was void, and the proceedings for temporary alimony could not go forward. But the Wayne Superior Court did not agree and overruled Walter's motion to nullify Lula's petition. The alimony hearing proceeded:

> Lula Odum vs. Walter Odum
> Petition for Alimony Filed August 22, 1908
> After hearing argument in the within stated case, it is considered ordered and adjudged by the Court that the plaintiff do have and recover of and from the defendant the sum of ten dollars

per month to be paid October 15, 1908 and ten dollars on the 15th day of each month thereafter until the final trial of the divorce case in Wayne County Superior Court.

It is further ordered that the defendant pay to L.L. Thomas esquire, the sum of $50.00 dollars, twenty-five dollars to be paid in 30 days from this date and twenty-five dollars to be paid in sixty days from this date.

It is further ordered that this decree be enforced by execution or attachment should payment not be made at the times stated. T.A. Parker, Judge

Lula's attorney, Mr. Thomas, may have portrayed his client as a destitute and discarded woman with no means to support herself. In addition, Mr. Thomas may have depicted Walter as a wealthy man who ruthlessly left his wife and child when he moved to Atlanta.

Walter argued that Lula had been unfaithful to him and abusive to their child and that those were the grounds for his divorce petition. But because the only eyewitness to Walter's claims of Lula's infidelity and child abuse was a lowly servant girl, Judge Parker would have heard a "he said, she said" argument. Believing what she said, Judge Parker ruled in favor of Lula and awarded her ten dollars monthly alimony, an amount equivalent to about three hundred dollars today.

The favorable ruling in the alimony case must have empowered Lula to fiercely defend herself when Walter appealed Wayne Superior Court's denial of his motion to nullify Lula's alimony petition. On April 16, 1909, the Supreme Court of the State of Georgia reached its decision in Walter Odum v. Lula Odum. With all justices concurring, the court ruled that "under the evidence submitted at the hearing, the court did not abuse its discretion in holding that the wife was entitled to alimony and attorney's fees, nor in awarding to her the amount specified in the order."

With his loss in the Superior Court, Walter's only recourse to end the alimony payments was to settle the divorce. And that day finally came over seven months later, in November 1909, when Walter departed Atlanta from medical school to appear before Judge T. A. Parker in the Wayne County Superior Court.

> Walter M. Odum vs. Lula Odum
> Libel for divorce Wayne County Superior Court, November term, 1909
> The following jury was impaneled and sworn to this case:
> W.I. Madray
> D.R. Thornton
> Henry Hilton
> S.A. Strickland
> D.L. Price
> W.S. Hilton
> Isham Roberson
> D.H. Roberson
> Cleo Poppell
> Bertie Westberry
> D.P. Taylor
> R.B. Wilson
>
> And returned the following verdict: We the jury find that sufficient proofs have been submitted to authorize the granting of a total divorce between the parties in favor of the defendant, that is to say a divorce a vinculo matrimonii upon legal principles.
> We further find in favor of the defendant the sum of three hundred and thirty-three dollars and thirty-three cents as permanent alimony. We further find in favor of the plaintiff the sum

of fifty dollars as attorney fees. We further find against the removal of the disabilities of the plaintiff. This 23rd day of November 1909.

It appearing to the Court that the Jury trying the above stated case had returned a verdict in favor of the defendant for a total divorce, that is to say a divorce a Vinculo matrimonii, upon legal principles. It is therefore considered ordered and decreed by the Court that the defendant be and she is hereby decreed to be totally divorced from the plaintiff Walter Odum and is hereby permitted to contract marriage again.

It is further ordered and decreed that the defendant Lula Odum do have and recover of and from the plaintiff Walter M. Odum the sum of ($333.33), three-hundred, thirty-three dollars and thirty-three cents as permanent alimony as embraced in the verdict of the Jury and the further sum of Fifty Dollars attorney's fees as fixed by the verdict of the Jury trying this case and disabilities of the plaintiff be not removed. It is further adjudged and decreed that the defendant do have and recover of and from the plaintiff the further sum of ten dollars cash for the use of the offices of Court in this case had and expended.

It is further considered, ordered, and decreed by the Court that this decree be enforced either by attachment against the person of the said Walter Odum or by execution against his property or both. Granted in open Court this November 23, 1909.

L.L. Thomas, defendant's attorney

T.A. Parker, Judge

If Lula's argument that Walter deserted her and their infant child and that his adultery claims were untrue worked in the alimony case, it must have worked again in the divorce proceedings. The all-male jury granted Lula an absolute divorce and ordered Walter to pay court costs, attorney fees, and $333.33 in permanent alimony, a total equivalent to about $9,000 today. The jury also ruled against removing "the disabilities of the plaintiff" and did not permit Walter to remarry. The court did allow Lula to remarry and it wasn't long before she did.

Lula, *left*, and Budley visit Florida with Budley's sister. Budley died not long after the trip in 1939.

CHAPTER 12
Winds of Change

AFTER WASHING OTHER PEOPLE'S clothes for four years, Lula realized she must again take fate into her own hands. Spending the rest of her life working as a humble laundress did not appeal to her. After all, Lula had been Miriam's domestic, and she had no intentions of being anyone else's for long.

Posing as a single, available woman three years younger than her actual age and dropping her married name of Odum fooled everyone. No one recognized Lula Moody as the scandalous harlot from Odum who mistreated and lost her baby. And because the divorce and alimony proceedings were in Wayne County, Lula kept her previous marriage a secret.

Shielded in her anonymity, Lula went after the most eligible man in Glennville, David "Budley" Beasley. If she married Mr. Beasley, she would never have to work again. But to attract him, Lula needed to present herself as a fine lady suitable to be with a man of Budley's social status. With the cash awarded to her in the divorce settlement and the money saved working for the Andersons, Lula purchased the latest fashions and remodeled herself into a desirable mate capable of luring any man. And it wasn't long before the one she wanted took the bait.

In December 1910, the laundress bid farewell to George, America, and their six children and stepped from one life into another. Almost five years after moving in with the Anderson family and only one year after her divorce from Walter was final, Lula Moody and David "Budley" Beasley wed. Budley was twenty-eight, and she was twenty-four, although Lula claimed to be only twenty-one when she married Budley.

The citizens of Glennville in Tattnall County remembered Budley Beasley as one of its most popular citizens, a man who made friends quickly and whose quiet disposition and genial personality endeared him to everyone. Budley owned large tracts of farmland, a store, and a grand home in Glennville throughout his lifetime. He served as director of the Canoochee Electric Membership Corporation and a member of the Tattnall County Democratic Executive Committee, where he and his family were active leaders. Attending church was most important to Budley Beasley; the Watermelon Creek Baptist Church rarely opened its doors without him passing through.

Long before Lula joined the Glennville community, Budley married the mother of his two children when he was eighteen years old in 1901. Budley and his new wife welcomed their first son, Jennis, in 1903 and another son in 1905, whom they named Buell. Budley, Daisy, Jennis, and Buell would have spent most Sundays at the Watermelon Creek Baptist Church with their friends and family.

Without the outpouring of devotion and support from its members, Budley may never have overcome the despair he experienced that awful day at the Park View Sanitorium in Savannah in 1906. Six weeks earlier, Daisy complained of discomfort in her abdomen, and when she could no longer tolerate her aching belly, Budley rushed her to Savannah for medical treatment. Given only pain medication while a raging infection multiplied in her body, Daisy never recovered from her illness.

It would be decades before the discovery of penicillin that could have saved her life. Daisy's death certificate states that peritonitis, probably from a ruptured appendix, was the cause of death. She was twenty-four years old when she died and left behind a grieving husband and two small children, ages three and one.

After Daisy's death, Budley and his little boys slowly adjusted to living without her. Four years passed before Budley opened his heart to another when he fell hard for Lula, the alluring new woman in town. If Budley had known about Lula's past and that she lied about her age, it is doubtful that he would have trusted her to care for his little boys. Ironically, the same year Lula lost Mildred May, Jennis and Buell lost their mother. Perhaps Lula believed she could achieve atonement for what she had done to Mildred May if she was a good mother to Budley's seven- and five-year-old boys. Lula may have fooled Budley into believing that she was a righteous woman, but not my father, Joe Hodge:

"I learned about the Beasley's when Hugh Love started working with me at Doctortown. He was raised above Tison in Mendes. And all the Beasleys owned banks, and they were all wealthy. One of them was a mail carrier, which, back then, was pretty high ranking.

"Here's the kicker: Budley had land, houses, and farms, and his wife had died, and he had children. How did he end up with someone as crazy as Lou? Well, I mean wild. Because she was still wild, and she cussed like a sailor. Irma and I used to visit Lula."

Budley, a man of faith, must have gotten a kick out of walking on Lula's "wild" side and overlooked her cussing because their marriage lasted twenty-eight years. Lula would have been an answer to Budley's prayers; she was youthful, fun, and desirable, and he was very much in love with her. And Budley was an answer to Lula's prayers too. Budley's love for her, his wealth and social status, his children, and his beautiful home replaced all that Lula lost in Odum.

My older brother Jody remembers Lula's house and country store in Glennville.

"I actually remember the house better than I remember Lou Beasley. The thing I remember about the house is the stained glass on each side of the front door. I remember it was predominantly red, and I would stand inside the house. I was only five or six years old and looked through the glass to see the different colors.

"And it was a standard-style house of the period. When you came in the front door, I think off to the right was her bedroom and off to the left was the living room and parlor. And then I remembered the kitchen was in the back. And she had a porch that went all the way around the house, as I recall. I don't remember any details about the furniture or anything else in the house. The other thing I remember about it so well is the huge, nice grape arbor, and it had the best grapes, really good.

"I remember what the outside of the store looked like, but I can't remember what the inside looked like. It was a standard country store made of unfinished wood and a front porch. My memory is that it had a 'Drink Coca-Cola' sign painted on the side of the store."

Lula's Glennville home and her Beasley family embodied a source of great pride for Lula, validated by her scrapbook that still exists today. Its fragile black pages are replete with carefully cut and glued newspaper articles that chronicle the political career of Budley's brother, John C. Beasley. One clipping describes John Beasley as "The People's Choice" and "Easy Senate Winner."

Lula's book of long ago interestingly also includes multiple clippings of newspaper articles that today would be enthralling *Dateline* episodes: "Glennville Farmer Killed by a Train," "Glennville Man Slain in Toombs," "Young Glennville Man Shoots Self." Lula's fascination with true-life tragic events is an oddity shared with her granddaughter, Irma, her great-granddaughters—I being one of them—and her great-great-granddaughters, all of whom are avid *Dateline* viewers.

Also, in Lula's scrapbook are photographs of men, women, and children wearing stylish 1920s-style clothing that I assume are Lula and Budley's acquaintances and Budley's family members. The pictures of Lula and Budley's large home, their automobiles, and their friends who lived in the '20s and '30s offer an insight into Lula and Budley's life of affluence and privilege. Notably missing are any images of Mildred or Mildred's children. There is, however, a wallet-size photograph of Lula's brother, Harry, that she enlarged and framed.

Mixed among the photographs and newspaper articles, one newspaper clipping in Lula's memory book stands out among the others:

> MOTHER ABANDONS NEWBORN BABE
> Tells Colored Woman to Raise it or Kill it.
> Darien, Ga. July 27—Sheriff A.S. Poppell was summoned this afternoon to Crescent, twelve miles north of Darien, to investigate what turned out to be a pitiful and sordid abandonment of a new-born babe by its mother yesterday.
> The story as told by the sheriff tonight is as follows: Sunday, about noon, a white woman appeared at the home of Jane Furferson, colored, near Crescent, and later in the afternoon gave birth to a boy baby. Although Jane claims to know this white person, she declined to divulge the name to the sheriff.
> She told the colored woman that she could have the baby. The woman replied: "I don't want it; I can't take care of it." To which the mother is said to have replied: "Then hit it in the head and throw it over the back fence."
> Later in the evening, the mother is said to have left the house and ridden off with someone who evidently came for her. How she was physically able to walk to the road and leave the vicinity is a mystery. However, leave she did.
> The colored woman then reported the matter to Mrs. Beacher, who runs a shop at Crescent, and Mrs. Beacher took the babe to her home and has cared for it since. The sheriff will make further investigation and endeavor to learn the name of the heartless parent.

Although the article does not provide the year of publication, it probably was written in the 1930s because of its chronological placement in Lula's scrapbook, long after Lula attempted to give Mildred May to her servant. The "MOTHER ABANDONS NEWBORN BABE: Tells Colored Woman to Raise it or Kill it" story bears a strong resemblance to Lula's failed plot to give her baby to a "colored" woman, and no doubt caught Lula's attention.

The article's account of another woman who did not want her child and handed it over to a black woman may have given Lula a distorted defense for her actions. Lula may have found comfort knowing that she was not the only woman ever to commit such a disgraceful, amoral act, although Lula did not succeed in giving her child away.

Since Budley was devoted to his church and religion, he may have disapproved of Lula's adulterous behavior but probably knew nothing of it when he married Lula. And Lula, who wanted no part of her previous life to interfere with her future, presumably remained silent until she could no longer black out the memory of that cold February day in 1906 when they took her baby.

Twelve years passed before Lula felt remorse for sedating and not feeding her infant daughter and, as a result, losing her. In 1918, thirty-one-year-old Lula had matured into a loving wife and a responsible mother to Budley's sons and was no longer the forsaken nineteen-year-old sent back home to Miriam. Lula was Mrs. D. B. Beasley, wife of one of the most prominent, affluent, respected men in Glennville. With her dignity restored and money to spend, Mrs. D. B. Beasley prepared to undo what she had done to Mildred May; she would take her from the Poppells and erase Mildred May's first twelve years of life.

But to get Mildred May back, Lula must tell Budley the truth about her past and the child she lost. Budley could have been upset and unsupportive but after seven years of marriage, whatever Lula had done in the past was more than likely inconsequential. Budley loved Lula, and he undoubtedly supported her endeavor to reclaim her child.

However, Lula miscalculated the bond that Mildred May shared with her Poppell family and they with her. When the Poppells refused to hand over Mildred May to Lula, all hell broke loose.

Lula appearing out of the shadows.

CHAPTER 13

A Blast from the Past

"When Mom was twelve years old, Grandma had the money, the means, and the brains to get my mama back. She filed a petition in the courts for the Poppells to give Mom back to her. She had the money to fight the Poppells, but they were not about to give her up." —Irma Hodge, 2006

ON THE 31ST DAY OF JANUARY 1918, Mrs. D. B. Beasley cruised into Odum in her black Ford Model T automobile, complete with headlamps, a windshield, and a comfortable leather seat. Twelve years had passed since Lula departed Odum in a rugged horse-drawn carriage, leaving her daughter behind. Modes of transportation had changed since Lula moved away, and so had she.

When Lula reached her destination, she stepped back into another place in time, unrecognizable. Once a shunned and ostracized girl who had been forced to vacate her home at age nineteen, she was now a thirty-one-year-old married woman possessing a confident demeanor and an air of sophistication as she exited the Model T.

Lula's purposeful, forceful knock on the front door pierced the tranquility of the Poppells' home. Caroline must have felt the eerie winds of change she thought might blow her way someday as she peered through the partially opened door and saw Lula standing there.

Caroline did not invite Lula into her home, choosing to speak with her behind the door. Before Caroline could greet her unwelcomed visitor, Lula shouted out that she was Mildred May's mother and reminded Caroline that she did not give the Poppells permission to take her child. Caroline advised Lula of Mildred May's condition when they took her and that Mildred May had recovered and flourished with her new family. But any attempt by Caroline to reason with Lula or persuade her to vacate the Poppell property proved futile. Lula did not back off, and the heated verbal exchange between the two women blared throughout the Poppell home. Unfazed by Caroline's explanation for taking Mildred May, Lula demanded that Caroline immediately release Mildred May to her.

No one in the Poppell family ever raised their voices, and the intense exchange between Caroline and the intruder frightened Mildred May. By the time Bell whisked Mildred May away from the arguing women in the doorway, it was too late; Mildred May heard everything. She heard Caroline declare that there was no way she would allow Lula to take Mildred May from her, and Mildred May heard Lula proclaim that she would get her child back one way or another as Caroline slammed the door.

During the first few years after abducting Mildred May, Caroline feared Lula might reappear. But it had been twelve years since they had taken her, and Caroline assumed Lula had no intention of ever coming back for Mildred May. But much to her dismay, Lula mysteriously surfaced from out of the blue, and Caroline could no longer hide the tragedy of Mildred May's birth and first few weeks of life from her daughter.

Lula's sudden appearance forced Caroline to explain to a very scared and confused Mildred May that the woman at the door was her birth mother. To calm her frightened daughter, Caroline promised Mildred May she would not let Lula take her, but Caroline may have made a promise that even the "Tank" could not keep.

Caroline would not have known that Lula had just begun to fight, and neither would she have known that Lula was no stranger to court proceedings, having fought Walter and won in court three times. Lula's winning strategy to represent herself as the innocent victim in her divorce case served as the same strategy against Caroline. Lula again assumed the role of a victim, this time as a helpless mother whose child was stolen from her, and painted Caroline as a meddling child abductor.

One month after Mildred May Odum's twelfth birthday and one week after Caroline refused to surrender her, on the 6th day of February 1918, Mrs. Lula Beasley stood before the Honorable Frank B. Jones, Judge of Wayne County, Georgia. Under oath, she deposed that the facts in her petition were true as stated. The following is the transcription of that petition:

> GEORGIA WAYNE COUNTY TO THE HONORABLE F. B. JONES, ORDINARY OF SAID COUNTY: The Petition of Mrs. Lula Beasley, shows unto the Court the following facts, to-wit:
> First. That your petitioner is the legitimate mother and sole parent of Mildred Odum, a female child of the age of twelve years, which is now in the possession and custody of Mrs. C. A. Poppell, a resident of said County.
> Second. Petitioner shows that the possession and custody of said child held by the said Mrs. C. A. Poppell, illegal and without custody of law.
> Third. That the detention of said child is illegal, and her possession is wrongfully held from your petitioner, she being her mother and is without her consent and against her wishes.
> Fourth. Your petitioner avers that she did on the 31st day of January 1918, demand the custody of said child, from the said detention of Mrs. C.A. Poppell, and she failed and refuses to deliver to the petitioner the person of said child, although

she was entitled to her care and protection.

Fifth. Your petitioner further shows unto the Court that she is able to support, maintain and educate her, and give to her able education, support and maintenance, and that said defendant who has the custody and care of the said child is not able financially or otherwise to maintain, educate and care for the said child, as the law requires.

Sixth. Petitioner further shows that said defendant is holding the custody and possession of said child illegally and without rule of law, having no right or title whatsoever.

Seventh. Petitioner avers, that said detention of said Mildred, Petitioner's daughter, is illegal, because she is the mother of said child and entitled as such to control, and to her services, and the proceeds of her labor, and she has not at any time by consent or otherwise released her right to possession, and custody of said child, to the defendant herein.

WHEREFORE YOUR PETITIONER PRAYS YOUR ORDER, to grant the petitioner, the States Writ of Habeas Corpus, directed by the defendant, Mrs. C. A. Poppell, demanding and requiring her to produce the person of the said minor to-wit: Mildred Odum, before your honor, at such time and place that your honor may seem meet and proper, so that justice may be had on the premises.

Signed: Jas R. Thomas, Petitioner's Attorney

In response to Lula's petition, Judge Jones issued the following writ to be served:

> GEORGIA WAYNE COUNTY To Mrs. C. A. Poppell, of said County. You are hereby commanded to produce the body of Mildred Odum alleged to be illegally detained by you, together with the cause of the detention, on the 12th day of February, next 1918, at 11 o'clock A.M., then and there to be dispossessed as the law directs. Given under my hand and official signature, on this 6th day of February, 1918.
> Frank B. Jones Ordinary, Wayne County Georgia

Caroline "Tank" Poppell prepared for battle when the sheriff of Wayne County hand-delivered a summons from Judge Jones "to produce the body of Mildred Odum." Columbus was too ill to escort his wife and child into the courthouse; he died less than two years later at sixty-one years old. So just the two of them, Mildred May and Caroline, arrived at the courthouse on time, 11:00 a.m., as ordered.

Caroline fought hard for Mildred May as she testified to the tragic events of Mildred May's first few weeks of life. She explained to Judge Jones that Mildred May was near death when she and Nina took her and pleaded with him to allow Mildred May to remain in her care. Caroline pointed out to Judge Jones that it would be traumatic and emotionally harmful to remove a twelve-year-old child from the only home and family she had ever known.

But it was Mildred May who convinced the judge that Lula should not gain custody of her. Mildred May was old enough to speak for herself, and when Judge Jones asked her if she wanted to continue living with the Poppells, Mildred May clearly stated that she did. After Judge

Jones heard Mildred May testify that she loved her Poppell family and did not want to leave them, he made the following ruling:

> GEORGIA WAYNE COUNTY Habeas Corpus, Before Honorable Frank B. Jones, Ordinary said County Mrs. D.B. Beasley v. Mrs. C.A. Poppell
>
> Upon hearing the evidence in the above-stated case, and it is clear to the Court from the evidence, that plaintiff by her acts and conduct had abandoned said, Mildred Odum. It is considered, ordered and adjudged by the Court that the custody of Mildred Odum is hereby awarded to the defendant, Mrs. C.A. Poppell and it is further ordered that the cost of this proceeding be paid by Mrs. D.B. Beasley, the plaintiff. It is further ordered that these proceedings be recorded as minutes of the Court.
>
> This the 12th day of February, 1918. Frank B. Jones Ordinary, Wayne County Georgia

"The custody of Mildred Odum is hereby awarded to the defendant, Mrs. C.A. Poppell."

Armed with only their affection for one another and the mighty "Tank's" willpower, bravery, and conviction, Mildred May and Caroline valiantly battled Lula and won!

Lula and Budley's home in Glennville, 1931. Lula resided there after Budley died until she became too ill to live alone.

CHAPTER 14
The Lights Like People Have

WITH THE SIMPLE STROKE of Judge Jones's pen on the custody order, Mildred May jubilantly returned to her forever family. After the lower court's ruling, Lula appealed Judge Jones's order to the Georgia Court of Appeals and lost; Lula's winning streak in the courts was over. Mrs. D. B. Beasley never attempted to seize Mildred May from the Poppells again.

Lula had foolishly believed that her money could buy back her child, erase the past, and undo all the harm she had done to Mildred May. But just as Walter's money could not buy Lula's love, Lula's money could not buy Mildred's affections either. And it never did. Mildred never showed any interest in Lula or her wealth, and she never accepted Lula as her mother or her family.

Mildred's only mother was Caroline, and after Caroline's death, Aunt Bell became Mildred May's surrogate mother and surrogate grandmother to Mildred's children.

All of Mildred's children treasured Aunt Bell. If Irma had questions about her family, she trusted Aunt Bell to answer her truthfully. So, when Irma noticed a hauntingly familiar face at work, she could not get to her aunt Bell fast enough to ask if she knew the lady, as she later shared with me:

"When I lived with Norma, I worked at the press at the shirt factory, and this lady pressed beside me; I was only about sixteen years old. And I swear to God I thought she was my mama. Norma had a car, and she and I went to Aunt Bell's a lot, and that's the first thing I wanted to know. And Aunt Bell said, 'Is her last name *********?' And I said, '*Yes!* That's her name.' Aunt Bell then said, 'She looks like your mama because Ronnie is her father too. She is your mama's half-sister.'"

Bell was only fourteen years old when her older sister Nina began talking about her friend, Lula. Hearing details of Lula's romps with Ronnie would have been like watching a soap opera, and Bell tuned in for every episode. Nina revealed to Bell that Lula was pregnant with Ronnie's baby before she married Walter. Nina was not too happy with Lula for dumping Ronnie and marrying Walter, and neither was Bell.

Everything Bell learned from Nina, she shared with her niece, Irma:

"But I remember Aunt Bell talking about Grandma, and she thought she was the scum of the earth because she was going with Walter Odum. Aunt Bell thought she was just despicable. She was so different from the way the Poppells were.

"What Aunt Bell told me was true. I would stay with Aunt Bell in the summers. I'd sit there spellbound with Aunt Bell talking about Grandma Lou. Little did I realize how important Aunt Bell's memories would be to me until I got older. I just liked listening to Aunt Bell as a storytelling thing. But I realize now that Aunt Bell's memories may pass down to generations to come, your children's children, and their children and on because that's a keepsake."

Aunt Bell never married or had children. Much of her life centered around Mildred and Mildred's children. She lived in a simple home given to her by her sister Izy's husband; she pumped water from a well, made her clothes, raised chickens, and planted gardens. Without any frills or excesses that money can buy, her simple lifestyle left her stripped down to the sweetest essence of life: family, friends, and loving arms to welcome all who entered her humble dwelling.

Bell dearly loved her sister Mildred and all of Mildred's children. But she never, ever accepted Heber, Mildred's husband. Bell remembered all the times she and Nina protected Mildred from Heber during the early years of their marriage. Bell felt nothing but disdain for Heber, and he showed no respect for her either. Heber attached only to people easily manipulated to use them, and Bell was not one of those people. Bell did not possess anything Heber wanted, but Lula did; she had money. My mother clearly recalled the day Heber contacted Lula when he refused to spend his own money to save his dying wife:

"Daddy had nothing to do with Grandma. He hated her. But when Mama had typhoid fever, he walked to Madray Springs to call her. There were no phones on the farm. And he called Grandma and said, 'If you want to see your daughter alive, you better come. She's dying.'

"Grandma sent an ambulance. Grimes Ambulance came to get Mama and took her to the hospital in Savannah. I guess that she lived because she received hospital care. A lot of people died from typhoid fever."

Lula sent the ambulance for Mildred and paid for Mildred's hospital care when Irma was five years old, not Heber. And although Lula's money saved Mildred's life, it did not buy her daughter's love or respect. Mildred never appreciated Lula's life-saving intervention and never had any feelings for her.

Only one of Mildred's children admired and loved Lula, her daughter Irma, my mother. Mildred's other children recognized Lula only as the villainous woman who abused their mother, and they never called her "Grandma Lou." She meant nothing to them, just as she meant nothing to Mildred.

But to Irma, Lula did mean something. Irma is the only one of Mildred's children who had a relationship with Lula. If Irma had shared her recollection of the tenderness Grandma Lou extended to her when she was twelve years old, her sisters might have understood Irma's strange affection for the woman they renounced.

By the time Aunt Bell disclosed to Irma that her Grandma Lou harmed Mildred when she was an infant, too much time had passed, and Irma could not disavow the woman she briefly lived with when she was a child. Irma searched her heart and found forgiveness for Lula.

Irma moved in with Lula in June 1939, a few weeks after Lula's husband Budley passed away. Budley's will left Lula all his household possessions and stipulated that she could remain in his home until her death:

> I give, bequeath, and devise to my beloved wife, Mrs. Lou Beasley, all household and kitchen furnishings of every character and description, and in addition to this, I expressly disclaim title to the Doge (sic) automobile now in our possession, this automobile having been given to me by my wife as a present several months ago.
> I give, bequeath, and devise to my wife for and during her natural life my homeplace, where I now live, with improvements therein, this same being a tract of land containing seventy-seven and one-half acres, more or less, and bounded on the south and west by lands of C.C. Padgett. I give and bequeath the said tract of land with all the improvements therein to my sons Jennis Beasley and Buell Beasley, share and share alike, they to take and have complete possession of the same after the death of my said wife but not before.

With Budley's passing, Lula became a very wealthy widow, but she was lonely. So, she recreated the arrangement made between Miriam and her when she brought her twelve-year-old granddaughter, Irma, into her home. Also, Lula may have tried one more time to make amends for what she did to Mildred May by giving her granddaughter the love and care she failed to provide Mildred May. My mother recalled every detail of the time she lived with Grandma Lou, and the "lights like people have":

"When Daddy rented the farm in Madray Springs and we moved to the Crossroads, Grandma had this gorgeous Victorian two-story house and store in Glennville, Georgia. And Henry Oglesby ran the store. His wife helped him and had two or three kids.

"Grandma came and said if they let me go and live with her, she would clothe me and send me to school, and I'd be company for her. I was in the seventh grade. Daddy let her do it. I don't know how long in the seventh grade I had gone. It must have been after Christmas, she got angry at me. I didn't mind her or something, and she said, 'I'm taking you back to your Daddy.' And I'll never forget it. There are some things in my brain that I won't ever forget, and things I should forget I don't. And things I should remember, I can't.

"That's when I had my first period. I can remember it like it was yesterday. I woke up. I slept with Grandma. I thought I had wet the bed. I had on blue flowery pajamas. I'd never had pajamas before. And big windows, she didn't put the shades down. And less than that house is from here, I could see the store and pecan trees through the window.

"And the lights, she had those lights like people have. And I looked down, and I was bloody all over. So, Grandma sensed I was getting scared, and I started crying. And she looked at me, and she said that's to be expected. Girls do that when they reach maturity or go through puberty or whatever she said, but she had all the stuff for me. Anyway, she cleaned me up, and I took those things off. I had really messed up the bed. She didn't fuss or cuss or anything."

Sadly, for Irma, the goodness Lula extended to her lasted only until Christmas, about six months, and then Irma went back to the farm where the "people" have no lights. Memories of the day Lula "brought her back" remained with Irma into adulthood and she shared them with me:

"Grandma said: 'I brought her back. She won't mind, I can't do anything with her, I don't know what's wrong with her,' or something to that effect. I must have sassed her. I probably did. I don't know. But I know I liked that lifestyle. I had plenty of good food, and she had a lady that was her seamstress, and I'd never had pajamas before.

"When she took me home, Heber said, 'Well, Lou, do you think she's pregnant?' Lula responded to Heber: 'Hell, I don't know what's the matter with her.' You see, she cussed like a sailor. She had a nasty mind. I don't know why she thought I might be pregnant. I didn't even have a boyfriend.

"I don't know how Heber said it exactly. This is me paraphrasing it. He said: 'If you think she's pregnant, Goddammit, you take her and throw her in the river.' Going back home, you had to cross the river. Mama said: 'No, you won't do that either.' Bless her heart. Anyway, Grandma left. I never did hate her for that."

My mother never forgot the time she spent with her grandmother Lula and the compassion she showed her when she needed it the most. And although Irma resided with Lula for a short time, it was long enough for Irma to develop a bond with her that Mildred never could. Living with her grandmother seemed like a dream to Irma and nothing like the nightmare that was her life. At Grandma's home, Irma had fashionable clothes to wear, good food to eat, a warm bed, and electricity for "those lights like people have"—and she had pajamas!

While she was with Grandma Lou, Irma observed a relative who was not poor, a relative who was intelligent and confident, someone she admired. Most importantly, Grandma Lou temporarily served as a mother figure for her adolescent granddaughter, whose mother was incapable of adequately supervising and guiding her.

Irma's grandmother was a source of great pride for Irma, and she wanted her new husband to know that Lula was a dignified lady who lived in a fine home, unlike her mentally ill mother, Mildred, who lived in a primitive shanty house. Irma boastfully introduced her grandmother to her new husband when she and Joe spent two nights of their honeymoon with her:

"I don't know how I stayed in touch with Grandma. I really don't. I can't remember. But when Joe and I married on a Friday night, my roommate at the nurse's home stayed with someone else, and I slipped Joe into my room. The next day, we went to Grandma Lou's and stayed Saturday and Sunday and then went to Savannah on Monday.

"Joe liked her. She was very cordial, a very smart lady. She was still living in Glennville in that two-story house, and still, at that time, she was renting her store. We enjoyed it. We really enjoyed it. She treated us royally. We must have stayed there Saturday night and Sunday night and left Monday for Savannah. [Chuckling] Yeah, that was my honeymoon because I had to go to school and Joe had to go to work. We must have gotten Monday and Tuesday off."

When I asked my dad what he remembered about spending the night at Lula's after he and my mother married, it is amusing that his strongest memory of his honeymoon was the bed: "I can remember when Irma and I spent the night there on our honeymoon. She had a high poster bed and the dern mattress was so high you could hardly get on the bed."

Irma's relationship with Lula continued until Lula's death, and her memories of Lula never faded. When I asked my mother if she remembered Lula's store, she said:

"Oh, yes! Very well. She sold everything from dowels to nails, but it dwindled after Mr. Budley died. Back in those days, when you had a store, it had everything from groceries to tools. It was huge. I remember it being huge.

"I remember Uncle Harry Daniel coming to the store when I stayed with Grandma in the seventh grade. I assumed that Grandma's maiden name was Daniel because of Uncle Harry. I also remember when Henry Oglesby ran that store. He had a wife and two or three kids. He started running that store, and it diminished, and it ended up being a grocery store. Maybe Henry was with Grandma in 1945 because Henry's wife and children were already gone somewhere. They obviously separated, and maybe that's when he got in good with Grandma. Because he had a good place to stay, and at that time, I guess she was well off from the store and the money Budley left her.

"Grandma and Henry would go fishing together, and it must have been on Sundays because of the store hours. I can still see how Henry looked. And there was no wife there. She had been long gone, obviously divorced and possibly remarried."

I asked my mother if Henry lived with Lula and she replied, "Oh yes, he lived with her. She had a lot of farmlands. I know when I was there, people farmed it. All I can remember was Henry running that store. He totally ran the store; she didn't."

Without Henry's wife and children around, Henry and Lula may have shared time together doing more than fishing. After all, he did reside in her house. No doubt he lived with Lula in November 1949 when he received a postcard from Wallis Oglesby addressed to "Mr. Henry Ogelsby, Glennville, Ga. RFD#4," Lula's address.

Attracting men had always been easy for Lula, and even in her fifties, she was still an appealing woman. When I asked my mother to describe Lula, she remembered that she was a very nice-looking lady who wore a size ten or twelve dress and was "very upright, not wrinkled with all her teeth." She remembered that Lula's hair was dark and that if she had any gray hair, "you had to look for them."

When Henry began working for Lula, she acquired the nickname "Miss Lou," the inspiration for my cat's name: "Miss Lou." Addressing her as Miss Lou may have been a sign of respect shown to her by her caretakers, or maybe it was Henry's endearing pet name for her. Recently divorced Henry would have relished the advantages of living with an older but engaging widow and especially admired the Dodge that Budley left Lula.

My dad recalled seeing the Dodge for the first time: "When Irma and I married in forty-five, Lula had a thirty-six Dodge that only had six thousand miles on it. But when Henry came into the picture, I think he put the mileage on the Dodge."

Lula and Henry lived together until she became too ill to remain in her home, and Henry could not or would not take care of her. Jody remembered that Lula was already bedridden in 1951 when she was sixty-five:

"My impression of her is that she was sickly, ailing, or elderly. I don't know how old she actually was. When we visited her, she didn't come out to sit and socialize; she stayed in bed. Well, that's my recollection of her. I don't have any memory of her walking around or doing anything. She was always in her bed."

For ten years, Lula was "sickly" and "ailing," and Irma was the only one who showed any sympathy for her during her final years. When Mildred asked Puddin if she thought she should bring Lula into her home to care for her, Puddin voiced a strong opinion: "You're not bringing that woman into your house and sharing your little bit of food with her. She did nothing for you." But Irma had a different opinion on what Mildred should do:

"Anyway, when my grandma got really sick in 1960, Dot Surrency called Mama at the housing project where she lived to tell her that Lou was not well. And I said, 'Mama, you've got to let her come and stay with you.' Mr. Grimes brought her there. Mama didn't like doing that. She never was close to Grandma.

"I can't tell you if my life depended on it for how long, but I got a hospital bed and put it there. But bear in mind, I worked and had kids myself. And Mama did all she could, but Mama never did it willingly.

Mama never had a feeling for her, and Mama had a heart the size of this table, but she never cared for Grandma.

"She got so bad that the neighbors would come in and sit around the clock. So, Dot would go once a week. She was a dear friend of my grandma's and had been for many years. So, I told her, 'Mama can't keep this up anymore. We've got to get her in Milledgeville.' To get someone admitted to the hospital in Milledgeville for indigent care, you had to have a doctor request admission and a lawyer file the application. So, Dot worked on getting the lawyer. Grandma died not long after that in Milledgeville in 1961. She was seventy-four years old."

Walter's grave in the Odum City Cemetery, Odum, Georgia.

CHAPTER 15

The Disabilities of the Plaintiff

WALTER'S STORY SHOULD have been a "happily ever after," one for enduring that fateful year of betrayal and heartache inflicted by Lula. But instead, it was Lula who rose above the flames of destruction ignited by her unforgivable acts and lived happily ever after until she was seventy-four years old, not Walter.

On April 11, 1911, one year and five months after his divorce from Lula, Walter graduated from Georgia College of Eclectic Medicine and Surgery in Atlanta. With his medical degree and Lula off his back, Dr. Walter Odum returned to the place of his birth and the town named after his father, Odum, Georgia, where he opened a drugstore and medical office across from the railroad tracks. During Walter's lifetime, it was common for physicians to operate stores for compounding and selling drugs to their patients, in addition to owning medical practices where they treated patients. Pharmacies did not exist until ten years later, in the 1920s.

Walter would have been touted as a success when he returned home, the proverbial hometown boy who "made good." No one in his family had finished grade school or continued their education. Dr. Walter Odum was at the brink of a very bright future, but before he could marry again, he needed to attend to a lingering matter of unfinished business, the "disabilities of the plaintiff."

Walter prepared his case one more time to be heard in the Superior Court of Wayne County to remove his disabilities. And at last, the court ruled in his favor! The timing could not have been any better; Walter was ready to marry again. Interestingly, the following document recorded in the Wayne County Courthouse three years after the divorce is typed and not handwritten as the previous divorce documents were.

> W.M. Odum vs. Lula Odum
> Petition for removal of disabilities
> in Wayne Superior Court,
> November Term, 1912.
> The following jury was impaneled
> and sworn to try this case,
> Ira M. Davis
> J. L. Madray
> H.H. Daniel
> D.P. Taylor
> Henry M. Boyd
> John Wilson
> D.A. Dent
> A.C. Kicklighter
> J.T. Young
> Jas. H. Nichols
> J.O. Stewart
> T. J. Dent

And returned the following verdict towit: We, the jury, find in favor of the plaintiff, and removal of his disabilities, and allow him to again contract in marriage this Nov. 19th, 1912. H.H. Daniel, Foreman:

> The jury trying the above entitled case having rendered a verdict in favor of the plaintiff removing his disabilities. It is thereupon ordered, considered and adjudged by the Court that the disabilities of W.M. Odum be removed, and

that he be permitted to contract in marriage the same as he did before his marriage to Lula Odum. It is further ordered that he pay into this Court the sum of $--------- as a cost for the officers. Granted in open Court this 19th day of November, 1912.
Jas. R. Thomas, Plaintiff's Attorney
C.B. Conyers, Judge. J.C.

On November 19, 1912, almost seven years after Walter discarded Lula at Miriam's house, an all-male jury this time ruled in Walter's favor and permitted him to remarry. The following spring, twenty-six-year-old Dr. Walter Odum married eighteen-year-old Margaret "Maggie" Dennard in April 1913.

Happily married, Walter began putting the pieces of his broken life back together while practicing medicine in Odum. But the lives of the hometown "Doc" and his wife changed dramatically in 1917 when President Woodrow Wilson declared war on Germany and the United States entered the First World War.

Two months after President Wilson's declaration of war, thirty-year-old Walter, along with all males in the United States between the ages of twenty-one and thirty, registered in the first of three draft registrations. Walter's June 5, 1917 registration card listed him as a self-employed, thirty-year-old, stout (a somewhat fat or heavy-build) male of medium height with black hair and blue eyes. Walter's draft card recorded his birthplace as Odum, Georgia, and stated that he was a self-employed physician and surgeon. In section twelve of the registration card, Walter claimed his mother and wife as grounds for exemption from the draft because they were solely dependent on him.

Although the United States military exempted Walter from service, he supported the war effort when he answered a call for physicians to relocate to Brunswick, Georgia, and care for an influx of shipbuilders and their families. In early 1918, Walter and Maggie departed Odum and opened a small hospital in Brunswick. Although the war ended a year after Walter moved his medical practice to Brunswick and most shipbuilders left town, Walter continued practicing medicine in his small hospital.

With a dramatic decrease in Walter's workload after the war, he and Maggie had time to frolic and travel during the Roaring '20s when they sailed to Cuba from Key West, Florida. They could not have known that the trip was their "babymoon" since they unexpectedly became parents when they returned home. In July 1927, Walter's niece presented her newborn baby to forty-year-old Walter and thirty-two-year-old Maggie.

They named their baby boy Walter Marshall Odum, Jr., and with the adoption, Walter once again possessed what Lula took from him more than twenty years earlier, a child. Walter's family, now complete, lived comfortably until October 1929, when the stock market crashed and the Great Depression began. Little Walter was only two years old when his father's medical practice earnings began to shrink.

An article published on December 10, 1932, in the *Pathfinder* magazine entitled "Slump Hits Doctors," states that the Committee on the Cost of Medical Care reported a rapid decline in doctors' incomes during the Depression. The article further reveals that even in the boom year of 1929, half of America's doctors' pay dropped to $3,800 or less and about fifteen percent of all doctors in the United States received less than $1,500 from their medical practices. More than 4 percent lost money. In addition, the article also reported that in 1930, the first year of the Depression, physicians' incomes decreased by seventeen percent, and "they have been decreasing ever since."

With large numbers of people out of work and unable to afford healthcare, Walter may have been one of the doctors who experienced a "slump" and struggled to keep his hospital open. And it is reasonable to believe that the reduction or lack of any income may have caused Walter's life to spiral out of control.

Walter's gambling addiction most likely began when his patient load dwindled, and he had plenty of time on his hands. Like other unemployed Americans, Walter may have found an escape by gambling in one of the burgeoning speakeasies after Prohibition banned alcohol production.

In the speakeasies, friends entered secret rooms after "speaking easy" the password to prevent law enforcement from hearing it. Once inside, patrons consumed alcohol, gambled, and listened to live music. If Walter were a speakeasy patron, he would have known the secret password or perhaps a secret handshake to gain entry. After entering, Walter may have joined in one of the illegal games to satisfy his gambling habit.

If Walter frequented speakeasies to gamble, it is doubtful he consumed much alcohol while there; Prohibition permitted a licensed druggist to dispense alcohol for "medicinal" purposes. If Walter desired a drink, he could order one for himself. But it was not alcohol Walter craved; it was one of the drugs readily available to him in his drugstore, morphine. Walter may have started taking the morphine innocently for a problem here and there but discovered that it allowed him to escape from the worries of having little money when it flowed through his body.

But there are adverse effects from morphine, and Walter may have suffered from some or all of them. Morphine addiction induces sweating, chronic constipation, nausea, small pupils, reduced sex drive, slurred speech, and shallow breathing. Morphine also produces uncontrollable cravings that demand its victims consume more despite the damage it causes to their relationships.

Walter could have tragically been one of morphine's victims whose marriage not only suffered but was permanently damaged. By the time he realized that the morphine was destroying his life, it would have been too late. Walter would have been dependent on it and unable to stop using it.

Walter's gambling, coupled with the morphine use, must have been more than Maggie could endure, and she may have had no other choice but to leave him. When the Depression ended and businesses were hiring again, Maggie found work at an insurance company in Jacksonville, Florida.

In 1935, Maggie, eight-year-old Walter, and a twenty-two-year-old female, probably Walter's nannie, appeared in a Jacksonville city registry living in an apartment. As an assistant secretary-treasurer for the Southern Industrial Life Insurance Company, Maggie's position would have provided her the means to properly care for her son and give him the stable life his father could not.

Without Maggie and his son, and too sick and addicted to persevere, Walter's life seemed to slowly extinguish. A few years after Maggie and Walter moved to Jacksonville, the Brunswick newspaper printed the following in 1936, when Walter and Maggie's son was nine years old:

> Brunswick, Ga., August 24. Dr. W.M. Odum, 48, a practicing physician here for many years before retiring due to ill health, died at his home last night.
> He is survived by his widow, Mrs. Margaret D. Odum, Jacksonville, Fla.: one son, Walter, his mother, Mrs. V.C. Odum, and two brothers, M.S. and Wallace Odum, of Odum, Ga.

Walter's death certificate states that the cause of death was pneumonia and heart failure on August 23, 1936. However, the cumulative effects of morphine, the decline of his medical practice, and Maggie's move to Jacksonville with their son could have contributed to Walter's downturn and early departure. Unable to practice medicine and cope with life without Maggie and his child may have been more than Walter could endure.

When Walter was only eighteen years old and accepted into medical school, his future was bright until he married Lula Moody. Lula shattered Walter's dream of having a family with her, and she tormented him for years in the courts after they separated.

While attending medical school, Walter appeared before judges three times in his quest to free himself from the woman who cheated on him and almost killed their child. What must have seemed like a never-ending process would have tried the patience of any man, yet Walter continued his studies in Atlanta undeterred by the ties still binding him to Lula.

Walter may have never fully recovered from his traumatic past with Lula and then from the Great Depression that robbed him of his income, health, and family. Ironically, Walter self-medicated himself with the same drug Lula administered to Mildred May.

But unlike Mildred May, no one could save Walter from death.

Mildred with her seventh and youngest child, Carl, after beginning treatment for her bipolar disorder. Carl died tragically in a motorcycle accident when he was twenty-five years old.

CHAPTER 16
A Mother's Love

WALTER WOULD HAVE BEEN a good father to Mildred, the child who shared his birthday. He loved her before she was born, even though she was not biologically his. But Lula's callous disregard for Walter and Mildred eradicated any possibility of a lifelong relationship as father and daughter.

Tragically, the laudanum Lula administered to Mildred killed more than the bond between Mildred and Walter; drop by drop, it stunted the growth of Mildred's brain cells. Caroline and Nina's abduction of Mildred May was too late to prevent the assault on her healthy brain.

The Poppell women could not have known that the helpless child they saved would suffer long-term effects from the drug Lula fed her. Concerned only with its acute repercussions, Caroline and Nina spent days and days rocking and caressing poor Mildred May as they weaned her from the laudanum.

The Poppell women did not understand that Mildred May's uncontrollable trembles, stiffening body, and high-pitched cries were all symptoms of neonatal opioid withdrawal syndrome. Their instinct to hold and comfort Mildred May until her screaming stopped and her body relaxed mimicked practices used today to treat addicted newborns. Caroline's decision to move a wet nurse into her home saved Mildred May's life.

For years, Mildred May appeared unscathed by the effects of the laudanum. It was not until she married Heber that Mildred began exhibiting symptoms of a damaged brain. Unable to think for herself or make any decisions without guidance from Nina and Bell, Heber easily manipulated Mildred and took advantage of her compromised mental state. And after Heber went to prison, Mildred entered an abyss of mental illness that worsened as she grew older.

Mildred's mental condition remained undiagnosed until she reached midlife, and a neurologist determined its cause and identified it. Before the appointment with Dr. Fincher in Atlanta, Mildred's children had no explanation for their mother's mental problems, and they questioned if they, too, would succumb to mental illness.

Dr. Fincher explained to my mother that brain development depends on a variety of factors in addition to genes. According to Dr. Fincher, the lack of nutrients in Mildred's bloodstream starved her brain and stunted its growth. In addition, he stated that the laudanum exposure permanently damaged Mildred's brain and contributed to an irreversible manic-depressive disorder.

Mildred's diagnosis answered her children's questions concerning their mother's mental health and confirmed the accuracy of Aunt Bell's account of Mildred's first few months of life. If Aunt Bell had not told my mother that Lula drugged and starved Mildred May, Dr. Fincher could not have accurately diagnosed her. Mildred never spoke of her abuse.

In 1915, Charles H. Fletcher, a seller of Fletcher's Castoria, published the following advertisement and warning in multiple newspapers throughout the United States. It was nine years too late to prevent Mildred's poisoning.

> "Don't Poison Baby"
> Forty years ago, almost every mother thought her child must have PAREGORIC or Laudanum to make it sleep. These drugs will produce sleep, and a FEW DROPS TOO MANY will produce the SLEEP FROM WHICH THERE IS NO WAKING. Many are the children who

have been killed or whose health has been ruined for life by paregoric, laudanum, and morphine, each of which is a narcotic product of opium. Druggists are prohibited from selling either of the narcotics named to children at all, or to anybody without labeling them "poison." The definition of "narcotic" is: "A medicine which relieves pain and produces sleep, but which in poisonous doses produces stupor, coma, convulsions, and death."

The taste and smell of medicines containing opium are disguised, and sold under the names of "Drops," "Cordials," "Soothing Syrups," etc. You should not permit any medicine to be given to your children without you or your physician knowing what is in it. CASTORIA DOES NOT CONTAIN NARCOTICS if it bears the signature of Chas. H. Fletcher.

At the time of Mildred's birth in 1906, it was common practice for mothers to give laudanum, also known as "mother's helper" and "the poor child's nurse," to their babies to make them sleep. It was a selfish act to free mothers from the burdens of caring for a new baby. Unfortunately, Lula was one of those mothers.

Lula was nineteen years old when she poisoned her child, still a child herself and unaware that the laudanum was harmful to her infant's brain. She could not see beyond her own narcissistic needs, so she sedated her baby to continue the lifestyle she reveled in before Mildred May was born.

Today, more than one hundred years after Mildred's laudanum poisoning, many new mothers and caretakers continue to ignore the dangers of sedating babies. And tragically, some children are dosed with too much sedative and die.

Madison Park of CNN, in an article entitled "Drugging Kids for Parents' Relief Called Abusive," reported that a court found a woman in Massachusetts guilty in 2010 of the death of her four-year-old daughter. The court sentenced the mother to life in prison after giving her child a lethal dose of a drug used for treating children with ADHD. Another case mentioned in Ms. Park's article involves a Montana daycare owner convicted in 2005 "of killing a one-year-old after administering a fatal dose of cough syrup to put the child to sleep."

Lula was not convicted of any crime and did not serve time behind bars for what she did to her child. Only Mildred paid the price for Lula's wrongdoing by suffering from the mental illness it caused.

I do not think Mildred knew that Lula abandoned, drugged, and starved her when she was an infant, but if she did, that would explain why she never accepted Lula as her mother. But I believe that it was not the woman who nearly killed her that Mildred hated. It was the outsider who mysteriously appeared when Mildred was twelve years old and tried to remove her from her home, the woman she definitely feared and never, ever wanted to see again. Memories of that cold February day when Mildred faced the judge clinging to Caroline and professed her love for the Poppells must have haunted Mildred her entire life.

Lula could not have known that attempting to take back her twelve-year-old daughter would ruin any chance of ever having a relationship with her. Lula would have naively believed that Mildred would adjust to losing the Poppells the same way she adjusted to losing her birth family. If she reclaimed her child, Lula may have thought she could erase all traces of her selfish, reckless behavior and pretend that she never deserted and hurt Mildred May.

But Lula could not negate the bond between Mildred and the Poppells or the damage laudanum and malnutrition did to Mildred's brain. Robbed of her intelligence and ability to think for herself, Mildred lived with mental challenges that rendered her defenseless against Heber's manipulation and maltreatment of her and her children. And sadly, when Mildred was finally free from her evil husband, she was not free from the demon living in her head or her memories of Lula.

One of the reasons I felt compelled to write this book is to rewrite Lula's history, to characterize her as more than a wicked woman who drugged and nearly starved her child to death. I wanted to understand why she harmed my grandmother, and to forgive her. I believe that the loss of Lula's birth mother and the absence of affection from her adopted mother scarred an innocent child's heart and created a cold, careless woman unable to be a good wife and mother.

I could not have known this book would solve the mystery of why Mildred's children did not inherit their mother's mental illness and why they excelled in life, and their mother did not. Until I uncovered the court documents that proved Lula was a brilliant woman ahead of her time, possessing the mental fortitude to ask for and receive alimony, my mother and her sisters wondered why they were nothing like their mother. Mildred's daughters now attribute their longing for better lives and victory over destitution and despair ironically to the admirable traits they inherited from Lula.

But "nature" would not have been enough to ensure my mother and her siblings' success; they needed "nurture;" they needed their mother's love. Mildred May Poppell Robinson possessed the kindest, purest soul. My mother and her sisters often reminisced about their mother's selflessness, and they never doubted that she loved them. If Mildred had not eaten and they were hungry, she went without and fed the morsels of food she had to her children.

Without Mildred's nurturing, gentle heart, her children could have grown into violent, abusive people, having only Heber as a role model. But they did not. All of Mildred's children bloomed into accomplished, stable adults. I Corinthians 13:7 succinctly describes the reason Mildred's children survived the horrors of their childhood: "Love bears all things, believes all things, hopes all things, endures all things."

After Mildred entered her seventies, her daughters placed her in a long-term care facility in Jesup, where they thought the nurses would monitor her bipolar medication. But unfortunately, the staff failed to dispense Mildred's medicine as ordered, and she slipped into a severe depressive episode and did not eat for days. Mildred's condition was so serious that her daughters admitted her to the Rehabilitation Unit at the Georgia Regional Hospital in Augusta, Georgia.

During Mildred's rehabilitation in Augusta, Frankie checked on her mother often and reported her progress in a letter she wrote to Norma in 1977:

> Dearest Norma,
> I wrote to you last week about Mom. Maybe you will have gotten it by now. Norma, Mom is doing great. Her lip movements have completely stopped. She is wheeling herself around in a wheelchair and stays up all day, other than a nap between 1 and 2 pm.
> There are three specialists seeing Mom. She says: "I know I'm better." We took pictures of her yesterday, and I will send you one. She asks and talks about you frequently. Please write to her as often as you can. She will probably be in the hospital for about 30 days.
> Love,
> Frankie

Mildred entered a second facility after returning from rehab, where the staff properly dispensed the medications prescribed by the specialists in Augusta. Mildred resided in several nursing homes without bipolar episodes until she died.

While in the homes, Mildred's daughters returned their mother's love when she needed it the most. Once a month, Irma, Frankie, Puddin, and Melissy, loaded with new clothes, powders, perfumes, and Mildred's favorite foods, checked their mother out of her care facility to spend a few days in a hotel, pampering and loving her. The precious monthly reunions with their mother continued until the end of Mildred's life when she died in 1980 at seventy-four years old. The sisters affectionately designated the weekends as "Love-Ins."

The Love-Ins created precious memories of the last years of their mother's life and reciprocated their mother's love. Love was all Mildred had to give them, and in the end, a mother's love saved them all.

Epilogue

A little red brick church with a towering white steeple remains on Georgia Highway 144 in Glennville, Georgia. Behind it is a cemetery that's been there since Budley Beasley and the other church members constructed the Watermelon Creek Baptist Church in the early 1900s. In 2006, I visited Lula and Budley's graves in the cemetery for the first time with my mother, and I remember my excitement at finally tracing Lula's steps in Glennville and thinking I should record my feelings and impressions. With a microphone attached to a battery-operated tape recorder, I spoke these words:

"We're at the cemetery behind the Watermelon Creek Baptist Church. It's Saturday afternoon, June 17, 2006, and it's sweltering hot. As soon as we walked up to Lula's grave, clouds covered the sun, and the wind started to blow. And I'm not kidding. It's cool, quiet, and lovely here. And right now, there's a welcomed breeze blowing, and we're in the shade."

I discovered the cemetery behind the Watermelon Creek Baptist Church fourteen years before I titled this book. I am glad I preserved my impressions of the cemetery and noted the weather. I probably would not have remembered that the wind blew as I approached Lula's headstone, and I would not have appreciated its significance. As Lula's much-appreciated breeze cooled my face, I continued recording:

"And right now, I'm looking at Lula's grave. It's left of Mr. Beasley's. His headstone reads: 'David Budley Beasley, born April 15, 1882; died May 30, 1939.' Underneath it reads: 'Thy life was beauty, truth, goodness, and love.' Engraved on Lula's headstone is 'Mother.' Under 'Mother,' 'Lula Beasley, no middle initial, Born May 5, 1894, died March 19, 1961,' is engraved."

As Lula came into this world shrouded in mystery, so did she leave it. The birth year of 1894 inscribed on Lula's headstone eliminated eight years from her actual date of birth in 1886, immortalizing her as a younger woman than she was, and I am sure she is most certainly happy with the "corrected" date.

Budley's son Buell probably erected Lula's headstone and would not have known Lula's actual birth year. And he would have endearingly added "Mother" to it, another gesture that would have also pleased Lula. Budley's son, Jennis, did not outlive his stepmother. At the age of fifty, he died in an automobile accident.

According to my mother, Mildred did not attend Lula's funeral or burial and would have never inscribed "Mother" on Lula's headstone. It is ironic that a woman who almost killed her only child lies beneath a grave marker inscribed with "Mother" and lived her life in wealth and prosperity while her only daughter lived in poverty with an abusive man.

I live about three hours north of Glennville and I try to stop by Lula's grave when traveling to the coast. After placing wildflowers picked along the road beneath Lula's headstone, I stand and wait for her breeze. When I feel it, I take a deep breath and think to myself: *Lula, you are not forgotten and you are loved.*

And then I make the short drive to the Watermelon Creek Vineyard located across the road from where Lula and Budley's home once stood. There's nothing left of the house or the store; only an overgrown corner lot visible from the vineyard's second-level, Tuscany-style deck remains.

The vineyard's owners are a kind, welcoming couple whose guests relish deliciously prepared meals and expertly crafted wines. When I stop by the vineyard, I ask for a table adjacent to the vine-covered arches on the upstairs deck. Before I sip my favorite wine, Twilight, I turn toward Lula and Budley's old homeplace, raise my glass high in the air, and toast the Women of the Wind, the women whose blood flows through my body and whose lives fill my soul.

Me placing wildflowers on Lula's grave in the Watermelon Creek Baptist Church Cemetery, Glennville, Georgia.

Mildred's oldest adoptive sister, Nina Poppell Moody, age: 39, and her husband, Sonny Moody, age: 53 in 1924.

Mildred's favorite adoptive sister, Bell Poppell, standing in front of the little white house I remember visiting when I was a child. Circa 1968.

Mildred's oldest children, Irma, *left*, and Norma, *right* wearing dresses made by Nina and Bell. Circa 1930.

Heber's grave: "Way over there" in the Piney Grove Cemetery, Odum, Georgia.

Heber's parents, Maggie and Monroe Robinson holding hands.
My mother said her grandpa Monroe was a kind man.

Norma and Tuff, the "horned" man, 1939. Norma was only fifteen when she left home and married Tuff.

Irma Gail Robinson's high school group photograph, 1945. Irma, *fourth from the right*, wrote her name on her dress. She lived and worked at the hospital when she stood proudly in the front row and stared into the camera.

My newly married parents, Joe and Irma Hodge, 1946.

Aunt Bell visiting Mildred in Jesup. Mildred is holding the child she was pregnant with when Heber sold the farm and moved his family into town. Circa 1948.

284

MARRIAGE LICENSE

State of Georgia, } To any Minister of the Gospel, Judge of the Superior Court, Justice of
Wayne County. } the Peace, or other person authorized to Solemnize:

You are Hereby Authorized and Permitted To join in the Honorable State of Matrimony _Mr. Walter Odum_ and _Miss Lula Moody_ According to the Rules of your Church, provided there be no lawful cause to obstruct the same, according to the Constitution and Laws of this State; and for so doing this shall be your sufficient License.

Given under my hand and seal, this 7th day of July 1905.

J. D. Crawford (L.S.)
ORDINARY.

I Hereby Certify That _Walter Odum_ and _Lula Moody_ were joined together in the Holy Bans of Matrimony, on the 9 day of July 1905 by me.

Arthur Johnson L.D.

Budley standing proudly by the Gulf gas pump at his general store. Note the Coca-Cola sign in the background Jody remembers seeing as a child.

Fifty-four-year-old Budley and fifty-year-old Lula posed for this photograph in 1936. Lula's look-alike, Frankie, preserved the framed portrait and Lula's scrapbook for more than fifty years and then gifted them to me.

Beautiful "women of the wind," my mother and three of her sisters gather for a "Love-In" in 1977. Left to right: Irma, Frankie, Puddin, and Melissy.

Acknowledgments

The first person I must thank is my loving, supportive husband, Charles, who never once complained that my writing demanded most of my time and left little for him. From reading my early drafts to brainstorming and offering suggestions, his support has been instrumental in making my lifelong dream to write this book a reality. Thank you, my love.

To my daughter, Stephanie Gail, my earliest inspiration for writing, thank you, "my forever," for being proud of your mama and believing in her. To Katie, Field, Tyler, Paige, Stephen, Gerri, and Harriett, I am thankful for your positive words of encouragement and for cheering me on.

My friend for life, Molly, thank you for having faith in me and motivating me every step of the way. I'll never forget the day we collaborated on the book's title and the jubilation we shared at our accomplishment.

To my aunts, siblings, and cousins, I will always be indebted. Without your compliance and contributions, writing this book would have been nothing but a dream. Frankie, Puddin, and Melissy, thank you for sharing your remembrance of the past and adding layers of authenticity and joy. Jody, Sandra, and Mark, thank you for enabling me to give our mother eternal life through her words. Cousin Charlotte, I am grateful that you share my admiration for our mothers' strength and resilience and that you had confidence in me to tell their life stories honestly. And to you, Aunt Johnnie, thank you for providing the missing piece of Lula's puzzle my mother and I could not find.

Joan, until you referred me to Martha, I had no idea where to begin; thank you. And I must also thank you, my dear cousin, for recognizing the value of our family's history and encouraging me to write this book.

Nancy, the book would not have been complete without your understanding of the importance of preserving my mother's stories. Mother trusted you with her painful memories, and you cared enough to save them. Thank you.

And a special thank you to Edna, Annette, Puddin, and Melissy for allowing me to use your photograph and forever preserve the memory of the BB Quartet.

To my publishing team at Constellation Book Services, Christy Day and Maggie McLaughlin, you brought the "women of the wind" to life and let them fly; thank you. And to Martha Bullen at Bullen Publishing Services, your careful guidance throughout foreign lands showed me the way with ease. David Aretha and Andrea Vanryken, the first to review my manuscript and validate its worth, thank you.

And last but not least, to my mother, the original "Gail Force Wind." I wish you were here. But I have felt you from above. I hope you are proud of what we have accomplished together. I love you.

About the Author

ANGELA GAIL GRIFFIN is a lifelong resident of Georgia, and currently lives near the Georgia Writers Museum and the Uncle Remus Museum. Three of Georgia's most beloved authors, Alice Walker, Flannery O'Connor, and Joel Chandler Harris, began their writing careers within twenty miles of her hometown. Angela finds it fortuitous that her dream of putting pen to paper to share the enthralling family stories passed down by her mother came true on Georgia writers' hallowed ground.

When not writing, Angela enjoys oil painting, sculling, and making music with her family. Accompanied by her husband on guitar and brothers on banjo and harmonica, Angela joins in on the autoharp and dobro. She believes the family that plays together stays together.

This is her first book. To learn more or contact Angela, please visit www.womenofthewind.com.

The shelter dog I brought home today understands the gospel. She's not a pure breed. Her ribs. Gratitude.

Made in the USA
Columbia, SC
18 October 2022

69601280R00100